Unleash YOUR INNER VOICE

An Introvert's Guide to Overcoming
the Itty-Bitty Shitty Committee

CATHY REILLY

Unleash Your Inner Voice:
An Introvert's Guide to Overcoming the Itty-Bitty Shitty
Committee
Published by Shine Publishing House
Denver, CO

ISBN: 978-0-578-56359-6
Personal Growth / Self-Esteem
Cover and Interior design by Victoria Wolf

QUANTITY PURCHASES: Schools, companies, professional groups, clubs, and other organizations may qualify for special terms when ordering quantities of this title. For information, email creilly@sharingtheshine.com.

This book is printed in the United States of America.

PUBLISHING HOUSE

To my daughter, Jackie, as my living guide to
help her be her own best advocate. You are so much
more than I ever hoped and prayed for, and
I am so proud to call you mine. I love you
to the moon and back.

AUTHOR'S NOTE

TO ALL THOSE INTROVERTS OUT THERE
struggling to use your voice, I see you. I get you!
I am you. Be brave. Never say never. Grab this book and
a tasty beverage to sip while you read it and be
open to the possibilities.

Chapter 1

INTRODUCTION

I AM AN INTROVERT.

If you were to meet me out and about, this might surprise you. I am a happy person and always wear a smile. My smile has allowed me to hide my introversion and my fear of social interaction.

When I was a little girl, my entire Catholic family would get together—aunts, uncles, cousins, tons of us— to celebrate holidays, birthdays, the summer. We would also celebrate Mass. My uncle was a priest, and celebrating Mass was part of our family tradition. My uncle went around "volun-telling" members to help with Mass, and he interacted during Mass by asking questions of the congregation in relation to the homily or the Mass. This literally made me sick.

I learned that if I avoided eye contact or ducked out to use the restroom, I was usually safe. Truth be told, the thought of speaking in front of a group, even my family, made my stomach twirl. If you took it further and forced me to have a conversation with a stranger, I would tell you to take a hike. Imagine how I felt years later, when I started my own business and began networking.

I still remember my first networking meeting at the Chamber of Commerce. Recalling it now, I can feel my stomach flipping, my heart racing, and my body sweating like a maniac (generally, I don't sweat). The room was filled with nearly sixty people conversing and smiling and looking totally put together. I entered and looked for someone—anyone—I knew. Nothing. I may have been turning green when a charming woman approached and asked if I was new to the Chamber. Turns out she was what's called an "ambassador," and her job was to find the newbies and make them feel comfortable. She led me to a glass of wine, and I knew I had found a friend.

How I grew up, the relationships of my past, and the fact that I was bullied in school made me hold tight to my security. Like a wallflower, I stayed quiet and avoided attention. As I gradually learned to embrace my discomfort, to use my voice—to leave an unfaithful husband, to survive a variety of health crises, and to face my own Itty-Bitty Shitty Committee, I found that being an introvert awakened amazing skills in me (like being a good listener). I learned to behave like an extrovert. I am and will always be an introvert, but behaving like an extrovert is a skill set an introvert can learn and master to shift her presence and still stand in her true self.

I know this: Being an introvert does not define me. In developing new skills, building my confidence and self-esteem, and learning how to engage perfect strangers, a new extroverted vision of me began to form, shifting my true self into something more.

This book is about my journey and the lessons I learned as I shifted into this new version of me. Whether you are an introvert, an extrovert, or something in between, you will find value in these lessons I share through my introverted eyes. You will walk away with tools to build your self-confidence, to find your voice, and to speak your truth.

I nearly lost my life out of fear, as I didn't want to ask for help, create attention, or be a bother to those around me. If my current self could talk to my past self, she would say, "Cut that crap out and get over it! Get over your fear."

This book is my legacy to help those who fear raising their hand or using their voice. This book is for those who fear attracting attention. I get you. Now get over it. Read on.

Chapter 2

BYOA
(BE YOUR OWN ADVOCATE)

OK OR NOT OK

It's five o'clock in the morning. My husband, Tim, awakens and takes to the mountains with our daughter, Jackie, for ski lessons. He's the cruise director, so he gets everything going. He prepares her breakfast, loads the car, and then readies her for the hour-long drive. I sleepily help. They are off, and I saunter back to my warm bed for a few more hours of sleep. This is my day. A day of nothing of great importance.

I am a wife, mother, employee, and new business owner. I'm sure you can relate to the business of wearing multiple hats. But on this day, I wear no hats. This day is about *nothing*. I wake again around eight o'clock feeling refreshed. I decide not to work out—that would require effort, and today is a day of minimal effort. I enjoy my breakfast and a cup of my favorite tea. Then I head to our master bathroom to do something extraordinary. I take an extra-long, very hot shower—get this— without interruption! Even the dog knows to leave me alone. The heat of the water dissolves all the stress and tension from my week. I breathe in THE calmness of A day with nothing to do, no appointments, no calls, no dishes, no cooking.

I shift gears and decide to give myself a pedicure. I admire my work. I collect the towels from the floor to do a load before planning the rest of my day. As I bend down to pick up the towels, I feel and hear a *pop* coming from my gut. I take the moment in and do not feel anything more. My first thought is, *This isn't normal*. I continue loading the towels in the washer.

Within the hour, I feel a dull, nagging pain in my gut. It feels like a big bubble of gas and the unmentionables. I feel the need for the bathroom, but nothing happens. I decide that heading to the mall might not be a good idea. I will stay home today and take a few gas pills. I lie on the couch to watch some slapstick humor. *DodgeBall* anyone?

I enjoy the brainless humor of the movie and head to the kitchen for another cup of tea. Moving unleashes a wave of nausea, and I drop to my hands and knees. *What the hell is happening to me? Oh no, oh no.…* I feel another wave. This time I am going to be sick. I am about three feet from the end of the carpet. *No, no, no.* I do not want to get sick on the carpet. Not the carpet. I really don't want to clean the carpet. *Crap.* I pull myself, arm over arm like a military trainee, to reach my destination, the tile floor.

The twisted humor in this act is not lost on me. I reach the tile and spew. *Whew!* I saved the carpet. *OK, I feel better.* I lay my head down on the cool, tile floor, and it feels amazing. I rest for the moment (OK, maybe twenty moments).

I get up and clean the floor. I do not want my family to find this when they get home. *Eww.* The medicine must be messing with my tummy. My sensitive stomach needs food. I clean the floor and debate with myself if I need to tell my husband about this. I go to the kitchen for food, and it hits again, another wave of nausea, dizziness, and disorientation. *What the hell?* Pain in my belly. Gas. *This is just gas.* I look at the clock. It's noon. *Do I really need to be worried about this?* I shake off the thought. *This is just gas.*

I want to try to eat something. Crackers and a soda sound good. I take a few crackers and a warm soda back to the couch. This time I lie down. *Oh, that's better.* The less I move the better I feel. *See. This is just gas. Nothing to worry about. It will pass soon.* Time passes, but the feeling of bloat does not. I try to use the bathroom again. *Oh, boy.* Another wave hits. *What the hell?* The voice in the back of my mind suggests something is really wrong. This isn't normal. I convince myself everything is fine. It's just gas. I am not calling 911 for gas.

I flash back to middle school, when I stayed home from school one day with pain that made me cry. My mother took me to the hospital, and we were really worried. After a few tests, they decided that my lower region was blocked and the pain I felt was actually gas. Talk about embarrassing! I tell myself, *I know what this is. I've got this. I don't need help. I can wait.*

At two o'clock that afternoon, the phone rings. *Oh, thank God. It's Tim.* I tell him something is not right, and I want him to come home. I lie still and keep watching silly movies. I close my eyes and think, *It's just gas. I am overreacting. I am just being silly.*

An hour later, Tim comes in, takes one look at me, and says we will go to the ER. I say, "OK, if you think we need to." My daughter comes to the couch and gives me a gentle kiss. "We had fun, Mommy!" I smile up at her. *She's so wonderful!* "Oh, good," I say. "Did you fall today? You know, Mr. Bubba says if you're not falling, you're not trying." She smiles and says, "Yup! I fell twice! It was so fun!" Tim scoops her away, and I wait.

Do I really need this attention? I feel so silly. He comes back in and helps me get to my feet. *Oh no, no, no, no.* Another wave hits, then everything goes black.

Later, my head spins while the Urgent Care doctors and nurses poke at me and move me and ask tons of questions. Another wave of nausea hits, and I cannot hold it. I shout, "I am going to puke!" I cover my mouth for fear of getting the room dirty. They thrust a cup in my face and I let go. "I am so sorry," I say. "I am soooo sorry." I cannot stop. The nurse smiles gently and tells me it's OK; they're going to give me something to stop it. I smile at her and say, "I love you, man!" She laughs.

The doctor reviews the tests and tells me I have a very high tolerance for pain. I shrug. He says I need to get to the hospital for emergency surgery. "You have an ectopic pregnancy and internal bleeding." Wait. *What? Pregnancy?*

I hear nothing else. Our daughter, Jackie, is the product of two years of working with infertility doctors. Even though we know how lucky we are to have her, we were trying for another. *Holy cow. I am pregnant! Woo-hoo!* The Good Lord is blessing us again.

I cannot wipe the smile from my face. I turn to Tim. "We're pregnant. That's why I feel so bad." The doctors fed me so much information that it all got very confusing. I got the part about eight weeks. "But wait, what about all these medications? Are any of them unsafe for the baby?" The room stills. All eyes turn to me and their faces go white.

UNIVERSAL SIGNS

I believe in signs. Whether we call it the universe or karma or energy or God, I believe our higher source sends signs to guide us in the direction of our authentic life path. I had been the recipient of one such sign and didn't listen. So, the Powers That Be sent me two more signs. Within two months of the ectopic pregnancy, I was hospitalized again, this time with two—not one, but two—detached retinas.

That was one of the toughest recoveries I ever faced. It was my rock bottom. It was the place I needed to sink to in order to finally see the signs.

Recovering at home from successful, yet traumatic eye surgery, one eye so swollen I could not even look in the mirror. I'm heavily medicated, with indescribable pain, and I see my daughter, and it hits me. This amazing young girl is now taking care of her weak and beat-up mother, her mother who could not call for help that day in February. Her mother who said nothing when she noticed the first sign of a cloud in her eye. Her mother who struggles with using her own voice and being her own advocate.

What the hell am I teaching her?

That day, a switch flipped. People make changes for two reasons. One is out of desire, and the other is out of pain or necessity. To be the mother I have always dreamed of being, I need to lead by example. If I want my daughter to be a strong, caring, confident woman, I need to be one. She looks to me, her mother, to show her the way.

I was riddled with fear. My biggest fear was that my daughter would turn out just like me as an adult, unable to ask for help, putting everyone else's needs before hers, being ruled by her Itty-Bitty Shitty Committee. My daughter is my reason for shifting into advocacy.

SELF-ADVOCACY

Being your own advocate starts with tapping into your True Inner Voice, shifting negative self-talk to positive affirmation, distinguishing between the negative and positive voices in your head, managing your Committee, and ultimately using your voice. As you learn these skills, remember that we are all created equal, but our experiences differ. No one is perfect. Embrace your differences, accept the differences, and you will learn to accept yourself, flaws and all.

Being your own advocate means taking care of YOU! Being your own advocate means being brave and asking for help. Being your own advocate means gracefully receiving and appreciating help from others. An interesting thing about someone offering you help: They offer from what is possible to give (from what fills their cup), and it might not be money.

WHEN YOU DECLINE THEIR HELP, YOU ROB THEM OF THE OPPORTUNITY TO GIVE.

As you learn the lessons of voice and Committee, you gain confidence, vision, and positive progress with your life goals. With each lesson, you bring value, just by being you.

Stepping into your own advocacy and taking care of yourself empowers others to do the same. When someone offers you help, take a breath and say *thank you*. Accept with grace and, down the road, return the favor. Imagine a world where we all support and help each other with grace, kindness, and gratitude.

My journey into wellness and being my own advocate wasn't easy. I'm sharing my secrets with you so we can work on this together. Our path will be to start every day with gratitude, embrace our True Inner Voice, speak positively, and work productively with our Committee (more on your Committee in Chapter 5). We will use our voice, face our fears, and walk away with gratitude. We will build our confidence and move toward the life vision that speaks our truth from our core values. We will pay attention to our progress, celebrate success, be brave, fill others' cups, and take time-outs to be sure our own cups stay full.

Chapter 3

YOUR INNER VOICE

FREEDOM TO IMAGINE

Do you remember when you were young, going outside to play with your friends? For me, that was before the time of technology. Cell phones and smart pads and Xboxes didn't exist. You simply went outside among the trees and bushes, and on the dirt or grass and played games like cowboys and Indians, house, fort, GI Joe, Charlie's Angels, and a variety of other good guys vs. bad guys games. You divided up into teams and created swords and weapons from whatever you could find. It didn't matter if you were a girl or boy, you would use your imagination to create a scene from a movie or TV show and play for hours. You didn't really think too much about what you were playing, how you were playing it, or who played what part. You just had fun. You created a story line, you assigned characters in the story, and everyone played their part, open to wherever the story took them.

And remember when you rode your bike or skateboard around the housing circle or neighborhood streets? Without much thought, you would ride over to your friends' houses and ask if they could come outside and play. Next thing you knew, you had a crew of friends riding bikes. You spent hours outside creating death-defying jumps and courses with hairpin turns, and you rode as fast as humanly possible. With each attempt, the crowd would go crazy, at least in your head.

As a child, I played with all the boys and the girls. I wasn't worried who they were, what their gender was, where they lived, or what their social status was. We just played.

Do you recall times like these? We were young. We were stupid. We had fun. No hesitation. No doubt. No fear. Just living life.

At that time in your life, only one voice rolled around in your head. Your voice. It was all about you. It was all about what you wanted. As you grew older and more mature, you had to live by things called *rules*. Enter the other voices.

The first people to give you a lesson or teach you something were probably your parents. Maybe one parent was more hands-on and taught or influenced you more than the other. My mother set the rules and boundaries and did the active parenting. She kept us in line, made us eat our vegetables, taught us manners, and demanded that we stay clean and act like civilized humans. Not bad rules, mind you, and certainly useful rules. My father was a different story. He was fun and, when need be, he was The Enforcer. When Mom ran out of patience, enter The Enforcer. We dreaded hearing her say, "I'm telling your father." When Mom got to this point, it was time to hide.

But let's not lose focus here. This isn't about the discipline. It's about the rules and living by them. Your parents were the first to create structure in your life. They were the first to tell you no. They set necessary boundaries to keep you safe. They also created expectations and rules. They taught you consequences. Your parents and these rules added another voice in your head. And so it began.

YOUR BRAIN'S DATABASE

As you got older, your world grew and so did the people in your life. Your world expanded to include neighbors, teachers, classmates, coaches, and friends. You had best friends, rivals, nemeses, and people who you swear were born specifically to bring you pain and frustration. As you entered adulthood, you gathered boyfriends, girlfriends, exes, spouses, coworkers, bosses, former bosses, extended families, and more. You get the picture. There is no end to the people in your life. Some of these people were very important to you and some not so much. As you live your life with others who constantly give you advice, make suggestions, dictate rules, give praise, and dole out criticism, the voices of people you find important join the voices in your head. I call that your brain's database. Here's the kicker: Whether the person is important to you in a good way or bad way, in a positive way or negative way, their voice is added to the database and stored.

Let's think about it differently. The database in your brain is a culmination of all the important people and their respective voices from your past and present. Some voices speak louder than others. As you can imagine, the voices from individuals and situations that are emotionally charged, whether good or bad, are louder in your database. As we face situations, decisions, challenges, events, and even simple tasks during the day, our subconscious thumbs through our database to find a reference from our past that can direct our present.

The older we get, the larger our database. The more people we are connected to, the larger the database. The more emotional the experience, the louder the voice. This database runs continuously in the background, in our subconscious, ever ready to pull out a reference when the situation calls for it. It's tough to make sense of all of the voices, especially if we are not tuned into our own voice.

You do you remember you have your own voice, right?

YOUR TRUE INNER VOICE

Your voice, your true voice, is all about you. Think back to when you were five and life was all about you. That voice in your head was and is your True Inner Voice. That voice speaks the basic needs and wants of you, what you hold important, and what you find valuable; it is tuned into what you truly need and want. As the database of voices play in your head, it's sometimes hard to hear your True Inner Voice.

When my baby girl, Jackie, was two months old, I flew with her to Ohio to visit my parents. Complete strangers would flock to see my baby. She was happy and cute. Each new person would ask if she was a boy or girl. You see, Jackie had no hair. Well, OK, she had peach fuzz on top of her head, so it was hard to tell if she was a boy or girl. As a hormonal new mother, this bothered me.

One day some of my family banded together to take my niece to the mall to get her ears pierced. It's a very big deal getting your ears pierced for the first time. It's nearly a rite of passage. This had me curious. I inquired if there was an age requirement for piercing ears, and there was not. The more I thought about it, the more I liked the idea of getting my baby's ears pierced to show she was a girl. My family had mixed reactions, so I called my husband. He didn't really care and said do whatever. Still, I had this nagging feeling that I shouldn't. Did you catch that? I had a feeling, a voice in my head, that said, *I shouldn't.*

Still, I liked the idea. My next move was to call my mom. Mom said that if she had it to do over again, she would pierce my ears as a baby, and she listed her reasons. Ha! I loved my mom's reasons, and I pierced my little girl's ears. It felt right. It was what I really wanted to do. I was happy, and my little girl looked like a little girl.

As I boarded the plane on the return flight, a familiar voice shouted my name. I was juggling Jackie and all our gear, so I was confused. I finally locked eyes with the gentleman trying to grab my attention. It was my ex-husband. Good grief! This was one person I did not expect to see. I waved and carried on with loading my baby and bags on the plane. Sure enough, as we exited the plane, he was waiting near the gate for me. He congratulated me on the baby and noticed the earrings. Then he asked if I thought that was a good idea.

There it was again. That nagging voice inside my head was called out, and I could put a name to it.

When I was deciding about my daughter's earrings, I could barely hear my True Inner Voice over all the other voices from my past. When I got quiet and contemplated what I really wanted to do, I could feel what was right for me. In the end, I made the decision based on my True Inner Voice.

I think you get the picture. When you face a decision in your life, in your day, in this moment, what do you really want? What do you really need? Your inner voice is there, speaking to you and giving you direction. You only have to listen. Sometimes it takes getting quiet. Easier said than done.

CANCELING THE NOISE

So, how do you get in touch with your inner voice, your True Inner Voice? How can you hear it above all the other voices playing in the database? First let me say that it takes practice and attention to tune into your inner voice. Let me also say that it is not hard. It's as simple as listening—really listening to the voices chattering in your database, listening and discerning what is your voice and what is the voice of another. When you identify your True Inner Voice, you find mental, physical, and emotional alignment.

Are you ready to find your True Inner Voice again? Let's start with a journal and pen. It doesn't have to be fancy or special; a simple spiral-bound notebook will do. Keep it on your bed stand, and before closing out your day, journal about what you want to see in your life. What do you really want in your life? What do you really need in your life?

That's a big, open-ended question, eh? How do you start? Start with something that has you struggling or feeling emotional. Maybe something or someone has been pushing your buttons. Are you wrestling with a relationship, a job, a house, a city, your finances, your health, your weight? What pops into your head when I say "struggle"? Start there.

Remember this as you begin journaling: You need to be able to hear your True Inner Voice. Find a quiet space where you can focus. Sit comfortably, close your eyes, and be still. Breathe. Breathe again. Open your mind, your body, and your soul to what you want to welcome into your life. Then listen.

The first few times I tried this, I didn't hear much. My inner dialogue was basically, *OK, I am listening. What do I really want? Wine. A nice glass of wine sounds good. Oh, wait. That's not what I mean. Focus!* I even wrote, "focus … focus … focus …." My next step was to make a list of what I wanted to experience. It was a simple itemized list, and it was a good start.

Don't be surprised if it feels clumsy at first. It takes practice to quiet your mind and body and clear out the chatter in your head. It takes focus to close out all the noise and listen deeply. This reminds me of a time when Tim and I were watching a TV show during our first year of marriage. It was one of my favorite crime shows, and he was in the habit of adding commentary as we watched. It was cute, and even funny, the first thousand times. He has a theory on the crime shows. The new character that enters the episode somewhere around the twenty-minute mark is the bad guy. Now, I must admit, he's generally right. (Don't tell him I said that.) But let's not lose focus. We were watching the show, and he was giving his standard commentary. When the show was nearly over, I realized that I hadn't heard a word he had said. I had tuned him out and had enjoyed the show. That's what you need to do. Tune out the world, tune out others' voices, and listen inside.

Listening for your True Inner Voice requires you to tune out the minutiae of the day, the people around you, all the mental chatter, and listen inside. Focus on your topic, your desire, the choice you need to make, and listen. Ask, "What do I really want?" Again, listen. Your True Inner Voice comes from your heart and soul, and it aligns with you emotionally, physically, and mentally. Your True Inner Voice talks to you.

In my head, I am a Chatty Cathy. I often have a mental dialogue with my True Inner Voice discussing priorities, values, and pros and cons. I ask myself, "Is this what I need and want?" Then I get quiet and listen. I hear and feel my True Inner Voice speaking and responding. You can do this too. Be a Chatty Cathy then listen.

TUNING IN

The best time to clearly connect with your True Inner Voice is before bed. Have your journal and pen handy.

Before you turn off the light and close out the day, pick a topic to focus on. Where are you struggling? Where do you feel a disconnect? What do you want to improve? In what area do you want more happiness? As you focus on a topic, ask yourself what you want and what you need. Focus on the question, tune out the chatter, and listen. Write what you hear.

I first heard my inner voice when the therapist for my first marriage asked me to journal about it. My marriage wasn't healthy, and the therapist asked me to journal about what I wanted and needed in our marriage. She asked, "If there were no limitations, what would your marriage look like? Feel like? Be like?" I journaled about respectful and kind conversations. I journaled about spending time together. I journaled about laughing. I wrote in detail about how I wanted our marriage to look, feel, and be. Nearly a year later I realized that what I really wanted and needed was not possible with my husband at that time. When I allowed my True Inner Voice to speak, I mentally, physically, and emotionally aligned with the action I needed to take.

As you journal about what you deeply want and need, get creative and tell a story. Suppose you are struggling at work: you're unhappy with the people, the job, the salary. Journal (as if there are no limitations) about a job that will make you happy. Tell the story about how your workday unfolds in this amazing job. Tell a story about your projects, the coworker interactions, your clients, how you feel, and how this job is right for you. Tell a story from your inner core; let your True Inner Voice speak and identify your core values. What makes you happy? What do you want?

The juicy part of gaining access to your True Inner Voice is that you make a conscious shift to think about what you desire. You focus on what you do want and need. What you think about you bring about. Focus on what you want to see, and you begin to see it.

Have you ever noticed than when you get a new car, everyone on the road is now driving that same car? What's up with that? It's the power of your mind. When you think it, you see it. You are paying specific attention! Those cars were there before; you just didn't notice. The same is true about your true inner needs and wants. As you pay attention to them, they show up. They were always there, but you didn't have access to them because you weren't noticing them.

I journaled for nearly a year before I got up the courage to ask for a divorce. As I closed the door to one love (albeit an unhealthy one), another love showed up. You see, in my journal, I focused on what I wanted to see in my marriage, in my relationship, in my husband. I would tell stories, list the desired characteristics, describe his charm and his personality—everything I wanted to see. As I got clear on what I wanted to see, I saw it. Another door opened and in walked my Prince Charming.

Maybe you're thinking that you don't struggle with any one area. You're happy with your life, your family, your career. But stay with me. First, congratulations! You are more in tune with your true self and your True Inner Voice than most. You're one of the lucky ones. Let's go a little deeper. Who or what pushed your buttons yesterday, last week, or last month? What happened that drove you nuts? What happened that made you lose your temper? Focus on that situation and journal about what you could do differently.

TELL A DIFFERENT STORY.

Describe a shift in circumstances where you do not lose your temper or feel your buttons are pushed.

My favorite question to journal about is, "If there were no limitations, if nothing was holding me back, what would _____ look like?" Fill in the blank with any area in your life—your family, your relationship, your job, your income, your next vacation, whatever. Tell a satisfying story about it.

Once you tap into your True Inner Voice and identify what you really want and need, you are primed to make decisions that align with your core values mentally, physically, and emotionally. As you practice listening for the true you, you will face tasks and challenges with greater ease. With each decision, you will lean into who you really are, listen, and choose what is right for the real, true you.

ACTION STEPS
to Awaken Your Inner Voice

- Put a journal and pen on your nightstand.
- Before you sleep each night, get quiet, focus, and listen.
- Journal the life experience stories that delight you.

Chapter 4

SELF-TALK

WHAT YOU SAY TO YOURSELF MATTERS

You got up this morning and headed to the bathroom. As you passed the mirror, you turned and looked. You couldn't help it. With that glimpse, thoughts ran through your brain. Chatter. Some of the thoughts came from your database as if on playback from your past. Some thoughts were from you today. What did you say to yourself? Was it nice?

I learned in a seminar that 90 percent of the time when a woman looks in the mirror (somewhat less for men), the first thought is negative. Is the study true for you?

Was your first thought negative?

Now zoom out to the big picture. If our first action each day is to look in the mirror and say something negative to ourselves, we set a negative tone for our day. Our brain doesn't decipher if it's true or not. The thought happens instantly, so we think it must be true. This is negative self-talk, and it causes us serious harm.

No one wants to start the day being told something negative. Would you say those same negative things to the people you love the most? How would they feel? How would you feel? Would they smack you upside the head? Would their feelings be hurt?

If you are a parent, imagine your children looking in the mirror and saying the things you said this morning. Would you want them to stop? Would you want them to love themselves the way you love them?

We all suffer from negative self-talk. We have terrible, hurtful, even mean conversations with ourselves. Most of the time, we are unaware of the negative self-talk happening in the background. We don't pay attention to what we say to ourselves. Our internal conversations become so habitual that they feel natural. We accept them as normal and as true. Left unchecked, this leads to problems.

I am a bit of a nerd about the brain. I am intrigued

about how the brain works and the science behind it all, and it's darned complicated. My love of the brain and behaviors started when I was in college majoring in psychology. During that time, I realized my limitations: Although I totally rocked at comprehending the theories, I struggled with spelling all the technical terms in psychology. Science was not my forte, and I won't use this book to explain the science of how our brains work. Even spell-check wouldn't fix my explanations. Instead, this book is about how to use to our benefit the way our brains work. My plan is to make you aware of the beautiful, complicated mess you call your brain, your conscious and subconscious, and learn how to shift just enough to create a better version of yourself.

INTERRUPT THE PATTERN

To make this shift happen, we need to interrupt our negative thought patterns. For the sake of this chapter, I won't focus on why we think what we think. Simply know that we do have habits of negative thought. Our thoughts stem from our subconscious and bubble up to our conscious awareness when we look in the mirror.

WE CANNOT CONTROL WHAT OUR
SUBCONSCIOUS THROWS AT US
AT ANY GIVEN MOMENT, BUT WE CAN
CONTROL OUR RESPONSE AND
OUR NEXT THOUGHT.

We can fight our negative self-talk with positive self-talk.

Next time you look in the mirror, whether it's first thing in the morning or during your day, listen and pause. What did you hear? Acknowledge any negative self-talk. Look in the mirror and say, "Thank you for sharing, but not now. Now is not the time to be negative." Pause and shift your thoughts from negative to positive right then and there. Look at your reflection, at your face, at your body, or even your whole self in all its glory, and say something positive. Positive offsets negative. Give yourself a compliment. Say something nice. Feel the shift from negative to positive.

Your compliment doesn't need to be fancy or complicated. Say something as simple as, "Great posture" or, "That color looks good on you." A great first-thing-in-the-morning comment to yourself in the mirror is, "I make this hairdo look good!" You get the idea. As you learn to pause and practice this every time you look in the mirror, you make a shift. You are shifting from negative self-talk to positive self-talk, no matter what your subconscious tells you. You are creating a new pattern of self-talk every time you look in the mirror.

Positive self-talk works wonders on insecurities. Be strategic with your compliments. Compliment yourself about an area you feel is lacking. Tell yourself that you are beautiful or strong or smart. Say how thin you look. Say, "Nice guns!" Strategic compliments and self-talk combat a whole variety of levels of your negative self-talk.

Recognition of negative self-talk patterns plays a big part in shifting to positive self-talk. Now step away from the mirror. How many other times during the day do you hear negative self-talk? If you're like me, you talk to yourself all the time as you are problem solving. All. The. Time. Think about the last time you were problem solving. What was the chatter in your head? Recently, a friend of mine wanted to give me a flyer about a workshop, but she realized she hadn't printed any out. She muttered under her breath about being stupid and unprepared: "How am I going to fill this workshop if I don't have the flyers?" I had her pause and talk this out. "Are you fearful of not filling the event?" *Yes.* "Can you give me the information on the event without handing me a flyer?" *Yes.* "Are you taking action to fill this event?" *Yes.* Together, we pinpointed the negative self-talk, paused, and shifted her thoughts to the positive.

You're savvy, and I know you get it. You can easily identify your negative self-talk. That done, can you pause and shift your thinking?

As I write this, I remember the conversation I had with myself on this morning's run. In my humble opinion, running is one of the highest forms of torture known to man. Being a person with legs like a Welsh corgi and lungs crippled from asthma and damaged from blood clots, I struggle to breathe when I run. It's hard to find joy in that. My favorite running song is "Misery" by Maroon 5. That said, I've learned to be comfortable with my discomfort. I've also learned that running is a great workout for my lungs and body. It helps me build strength and endurance. And I've learned that if I shift my viewpoint to accept the workout as it is (a workout, not pure torture), I free my mind for better focus.

This morning, I followed the steps above. I recognized the conversation and owned it. I told myself, "OK, interesting, thanks for sharing, but not now. Now is the time to focus on something positive." As my rhythm matched the beat of the music, I was able to tune out the chatter and negative talk and use that time to talk to God and problem-solve. I lost myself in thought, and time flew by. Suddenly, my workout was over, and my problem was solved.

PAY ATTENTION

I invite you to pay attention to the conversations in your head when you look in the mirror and throughout the day. Some conversations will be good, productive even. Some conversations will be negative, hurtful, and mean. Pause when you become aware of your negative self-talk. Recognize it for what it is—a thought. Thoughts are not truths. Acknowledge the negative self-talk and say, "OK, thank you for sharing, but not now." Shift your thoughts from the negative to the positive. Hear the positive thought. Feel the positive thought. Feel the shift.

As you pay attention to the conversations you have with yourself, you more easily recognize your negative self-talk and shift into the positive. You feel a shift in your energy, your confidence, and your productivity. You become a truer version of you. Your shift enhances your ability to deal with your Committee. Keep reading to find out how.

ACTION STEPS
to Shift Your Self-Talk

- Pay attention to what you say to yourself.

- Acknowledge the negative self-talk and think, "Interesting. Thanks for sharing, but not now."

- Follow up the negative talk with positive talk.

Chapter 5

THE ITTY-BITTY SHITTY COMMITTEE

REFLECTION

Do you remember in middle school or high school being compared to your friends? Your parents might have identified one or two of your friends who were "troublemakers," and they didn't want you hanging out with them. They said things like, "Do you want to end up like Joe's brother?" Or worse, "Show me your friends, and I'll show you your future." I heard, "Show me your friends, and I will show you who you are." As much as I didn't like hearing it, the truth is that the people you surround yourself with are a reflection on you and of you.

In my adult wisdom, I now say those same things. Show me your friends, and I'll show you your future. Show me your friends, and I will show you who you really are. The people who surround you, the people with whom you spend the majority of your time, are shaping you and are a reflection of you.

My daughter, Jackie, was in a second-grade school play about a day in the life of a bug. Every child had a role to play and a line or two to memorize, along with movements, dances, and scenes. Every child wore adorable, oversize costumes making them butterflies, bees, lady bugs, and other charming critters. My daughter was thrilled to be in the play. My husband and I took an active role to help her rehearse, our way of encouraging her to use her voice (even if we didn't use those words), and build her confidence so that, when it was her time to approach the microphone, she spoke with clarity and energy, and the audience heard her clearly. On performance night, she was more excited than nervous. And even though I gave birth to this child and hold absolute bias, I must say she performed brilliantly. When it was all over, she lit up the room with her beam of pride and confidence.

Months later after school ended, my parents came from the Midwest to visit with us in Colorado for a few weeks. They did this a few times a year to spend quality time with our family. But who am I kidding? They came to spend time with their granddaughter. Jackie shared her excitement about the play, showed pictures and videos of her performance, and recapped scenes; immersing herself in the play had positively shaped her.

MY STORY

Jackie's experience brought to mind the time I played the lead in my school play, *Oklahoma!* I was eleven years old and had never heard of the play. As an introvert, let me tell you, I found the whole idea terrifying. The scripts for the play were in this large black notebook with all the lines broken down for each character. There was so much! All the students got a notebook, and everyone had to audition for a part in the play. We were required to try. The teachers from our grade were tasked with assigning students for each part. We had to be willing to learn the lines, rehearse, and perform for the school and our families. No exceptions. *Gulp*. Even though I was terrified, I took it seriously and practiced my lines for the audition. In the end, I was selected to play the lead of Laurey. Me!

I was terrified and excited at once. I rehearsed my part diligently and put my heart and soul into the play.

There was no budget for costumes, and I recall digging through Mom's closet to find items that would work for the period. Just like Jackie, I found the night of the play to be exciting and terrifying and electric with energy. The play came off with only a few hiccups, and when all was said and done, the audience gave a standing ovation.

I shared this story with Jackie, and I could see the surprise and joy in her eyes and on my husband's face. I am an introvert, remember. I joked with her that she gets her acting talents from her mother. I turned to my parents and asked if they remembered that night, hoping they could add to the story and fill in some blanks. They both stared at me with vacant looks and said they had no idea what I was talking about. They didn't remember it at all.

I share these stories with you to reinforce my point. The middle school version of me grew up the oldest daughter of four children at home. Life was busy with both parents working, household chores, community activities, extended family activities, scouting, sports, and the everyday family hustle. And although the play was important to me, the bustle of life and having few friends made this event just one of a handful that week, drawing little attention. My effort hadn't been realized, recognized, celebrated, or honored by anyone around me, so its impact on me was minimized.

In that moment with my daughter, I realized part of what I missed growing up. My parents, who provided so much value to my life and created a loving home, may not have had the opportunity to encourage, support, and celebrate their sensitive and introverted girl to find and use her voice. Looking back I know this was not intentional on their part, still I never learned to use my voice.

That second-grade version of Jackie, with people around her to encourage, support, and celebrate her, has excelled in sports, academics, and various leadership roles. She uses her voice on a regular basis and as her mother, I am very proud. (Most of the time.)

COMMITTEE OF INFLUENCE

People and events from the past (like this play) are stored in our memory and continue to influence us. The people who were around you, especially those you perceive as important or valuable, continue to influence your decisions in life and business years later. Their thoughts, their words, their opinions are stored in your database and become part of your subconscious. The same is true for the people in your life right now. Those people around you today influence your decision making.

Said another way, the people around you, from your past and present, are influencers in your world, in your life, in the choices you make. Your True Inner Voice mixes with their voices to become the muddled chatter in your head. The influencers from your past and present guide your choices in life, in your relationships, about money, and even in business. I call these influencers your Committee. Simply put, the voices are the chatter and the people are the Committee.

Committee members who are stronger influencers are those with whom you have an emotional connection and an emotional memory, good or bad. When you feel emotion, your subconscious gives it extra value and power over you. Their associated chatter becomes louder. This event, this person, this voice can pop back from your subconscious in a heartbeat when you are triggered by that emotion. For instance, I worked for an attorney who made it clear he didn't want me on his team. It didn't take me long to figure out that every time I was called into his office, I had done something wrong. Being called into the boss's office triggered a negative emotion for me. For years moving forward, every time I was unexpectedly called into the boss's office, my first thought was, *What did I do wrong?*

Your Committee is a collection of your past and present influencers. That being said, it is a collection of not only your biggest supporters, your biggest fans, and your cheerleaders, but also of your loudest critics, your Debbie Downers, and your naysayers. When your Committee's chatter is more negative than positive, your Committee becomes the Itty-Bitty Shitty Committee.

Oh, the Itty-Bitty Shitty Committee is brutal and mean. Their negative voices and messages come flooding back when we struggle. What challenge did you face yesterday? Last week? Last month? Did you hear the voices? Were they mean? Our Committee can crush our dreams, if we let it.

MY STORY

One of my memorable Itty-Bitty Shitty Committee experiences involved running. You might remember how much I l-o-v-e to run (insert sarcastic sneer here). Although I am not a fast runner, I do love how it strengthens my body and lungs. A few years ago, I partnered with a friend and a team to run a half marathon. With the help of my team, I developed and implemented a plan. My first day of training was a twenty-minute walk/run pace. (I love training by time rather than miles.) During my twenty minutes, my Committee was in full session, megaphone loud. As you might have guessed, the Committee in session was my Itty-Bitty Shitty Committee. They were shouting in my head: *What the hell are you doing? You can't run! You look stupid. What were you thinking? You suck! You're not an athlete. You have no coordination. Even your ex said you can't run. You're a dork. Was that a lung you just coughed up? Do you hear yourself breathe? Are you for real? You're too fat. You're out of shape. You should stop now! Just quit. You know how to quit.* Blah … blah … blah …

Ouch, right? When the Committee in our head is the Itty-Bitty Shitty Committee based on negative influencers from our past, do you think that leaves a mark? Do you think it influences our direction, our choices, our decisions? Absolutely.

Here's a get-real question for you. Today as you read this, who sits at your Committee table? Who are the influencers from your past and present, both positive and negative, that shaped the you of today? Can you identify them? Way too many people sat at my Committee table. It's been said that if you stand for nothing, you fall for anything. That was me. I let others be my authority, and that gave them space at my table.

YOU HAVE THE POWER

Your Committee is what it is. Your people, your influencers, your family, your past experiences are sitting at your table. Good or bad, your Committee has helped shape the you of today. You sit at the head of the Committee table, and you have the power to change your Committee members. You have the ability to assemble a Committee that reflects your core values, your desires, and your goals. You have the ability to staff a Committee that aligns with your True Inner Voice, your true self. You even have the power to limit the voices of your Itty-Bitty Shitty Committee.

Your power comes from first paying attention to the negative thinking and then making a shift from negative to positive. Just like shifting your negative self-talk to positive, you need to pay attention to the negative Committee chatter and pause.

YOU CANNOT SHIFT WHAT YOU DON'T NOTICE, SO PAYING ATTENTION IS ESSENTIAL.

Pay attention to the negative chatter and recognize it for what it is—chatter. Once you recognize and pause, the shift can happen.

As you pay attention and recognize the negative Committee chatter, say, "Thank you for popping up, but not now." This chatter isn't valid. Just because you think it doesn't make it true. Shift the negative thought to a positive one. What you tell yourself every day is paramount to living a positive and healthy life. What you allow your Committee to tell you is equally important. We must pay attention to the voices, the chatter, the Committee, and our core values, and then shift into the positive. It is simple, but it takes focus.

I applied this process to my running. After listening to my Itty-Bitty Shitty Committee for the first part of my run, I paused and said, "Thank you, but not now." I identified my perceived influencer from my past and said, "Nope, not now. This opinion isn't valid. This opinion isn't real. I am a runner. I am strong. I can do this. I've got this."

Your Committee is what it is, and there is another way to create a Committee that aligns with your inner voice, your core values, and your true self. That way is to pay attention to the people in your life. Who do you spend the most time with? Who are the top five or ten people in your life today? What are their values? Do you get along with them? Do they make you smile? Do they make you cry? Do they support you? Do they lift you? Or do they suck the life out of you?

Let's make it simple. Make a list of the people in your life you spend a significant amount of time with on a daily or weekly basis. Divide a piece of paper into two columns. Title one column "Brings Me Up" and the other "Brings Me Down." Place the people in your life in the column where they fit.

If you are not spending time with people who lift, inspire, challenge, and support you, people who make you a better version of you, then it's time to make a change. You absolutely need to surround yourself with people who help, support, encourage, and inspire you in order to have a supported and inspired life. These are your peeps. These are the people who help you align with your goals and dreams then move forward.

If there aren't people in your life who fit this category, go find them. Join a club or group that aligns with your goals and interests. Meet new people. Start building relationships with others who share your dreams, your goals, and your faith, and who are in alignment with your core values and true self. If you already have people like that in your life, start spending more time with them. Ask them to lunch and seek their guidance. As you spend more time with them, you build positive relationships and you build a positive Committee.

Adjust your list so the "Up" column of your list is loaded and the "Down" column is minimal.

BOUNDARIES

Let's be realistic; not everyone in your life will support you and be on your "Up" list. Not everyone in your life will be a cheerleader and a positive influence. Some people in your life right now are Negative Nellies, Debbie Downers, and Energy Vampires. There are people in your life who have no filter and cause fracture at every turn. Let me be clear: I am NOT saying you need to cut them out of your life or go get a divorce. I am saying you need to be aware of the negative influence and be strategic about how much time you spend with them.

CREATE BOUNDARIES AND LIMIT
CONVERSATIONS WITH PEOPLE
WHO ARE NEGATIVE.

I've found it valuable to set some ground rules for the negative people in my life—at least in my head. Establish boundaries and limit conversations. Limit the amount of time you spend with them. By erecting boundaries, you are saying no to the negative and yes to the positive. (By the way, not everyone in your life needs to know about everything in your life.)

If you are in growth mode, personally or professionally, it's also important to spend time with people who impress you, are more successful than you, are smarter than you, and really challenge you.

Moving forward with your personal and professional relationships, be mindful of your daily conversations. Be mindful of their influence and your perception of their value. Be mindful of any boundary. When you pay attention, when you recognize the negative, when you pause, and when you shift to the positive, you gain power over your surroundings and the Negative Nellies in your life. When conversations take a negative turn, you use your voice and say, "That's interesting. Thanks for sharing. What I really want to talk about is …."

Your Committee is you, your influencers, and your past. These lessons I share can help you gain power over your Itty-Bitty Shitty Committee and create a new

Committee that is supportive, positive, and in complete alignment with your core values. I'm not going to sugar-coat it. It's work. It's not easy. But it's so powerful! Like Dorothy learned in the *Wizard of Oz*, "You've always had the power."

Let the shift begin! If using your voice is a struggle, you'll like the next chapter.

ACTION STEPS
to Silence the Itty-Bitty Shitty Committee

- Pay attention to those around you.

- Recognize the positive influencers. Spend more time with them.

- Recognize the negative influencers. Limit your time with them.

- When the Itty-Bitty Shitty Committee is in session, pause and shift.

Chapter 6

SPEAK YOUR TRUTH

SILENCING MY VOICE

I am a good listener. It's a nice perk of being an introvert. I use my ears more than my mouth. It's a skill I have embraced and used most of my life. At a young age, I became so good at hearing what everyone else wanted to do and everyone else's opinion over and above my own voice that I went along for the ride. I am also a morning person. And I am a happy person. That's part of the reason people don't believe I am an introvert. I am a happy introvert. And when you combine a morning person and a happy person, you are greeted with a smile and a *Good morning* to start the day.

Enter my housemates. In my senior year at college, I shared a three-bedroom duplex with three friends who were not morning people. In fact, they were quite the opposite and preferred silence in the morning. Early in our living arrangement they established certain rules for me to follow in the morning. I was not allowed to speak to them until they spoke to me first. I was not allowed to smile, make eye contact, or interact in any way until they interacted with me.

Because I was such a good listener and I worried about being a bother to them, I kept my mouth shut and followed their rules. Here I was, excited to be in my first independent space, yet I was living by a rule that diminished the real me.

I had every intention of going to law school and becoming a lawyer. My uncle was an attorney (and later a judge) in Ohio. Every time I saw him at family gatherings—I mean *every single time*—he asked why I wasn't in school. He was the first person to tell me I could be a lawyer, and he encouraged me to get a higher education. His words stayed with me for many years, and I was the first in my family to graduate college. I graduated with a degree in psychology with a minor in business, concentrating in law. After graduation, I decided to work and pay off my student loans before heading to law school.

Fast-forward to my first real job. I was scooped up by a growing law firm who loved the idea of paying me—a well-educated lawyer in the making—a paltry sum to work as a paralegal. The first year I kept my head down, kept my mouth shut, and worked my butt off as I learned the trade. At the end of my first year, my colleagues and peers evaluated me. I was still learning my position and had completed all my assignments. I had met deadlines and brought support to the team. The cumulative report from the handful of people who reviewed and evaluated me stopped my heart. My overall score averaged 2.5 out of a possible 10. Not pretty. We proceeded with the evaluation and reviewed the written comments. It only got worse. In fact, one attorney wrote that I had no idea what I was doing and should be replaced by a trained professional ASAP.

As you can guess, my head swirled with questions, thoughts, arguments, and emotions. I asked myself, *What the hell am I doing here?* How could everyone think this way? Did I not just work my butt off? I fought back tears and held my breath. I was given an opportunity to respond or ask questions, but I spoke not a word. I fell silent. I accepted their words without voicing objection.

The attorney who had hired me responded that it was the firm's job to train me, and I had done a good job so far. He recommended continued training and reevaluation in a year. As we walked out, he pulled me aside and said that was one of the toughest evaluations in his history. "So, look at it this way—you got that over with! Keep doing what you're doing." I did just that. I continued to work hard and with each passing year, my evaluation score improved.

We start off as youngsters and are told to be quiet or not be too loud. In kindergarten we are taught to focus on the work, the project, or the task at hand and keep quiet. We are instructed to use our inside voices. We are told not to disturb our classmates. And young girls are taught to play supportive roles, to help out with this or that, and to not make a fuss. Knowing this, it doesn't surprise me that I embraced being an introvert. I embraced silencing my voice.

No matter your upbringing, whether you are a man or woman, and whatever your confidence level, you have likely faced times when you embraced the quiet and stifled your voice. Even if you are not an introvert, I bet you can still think of a time that you chose to stay quiet and not speak up. You found comfort in keeping your mouth shut.

Nearly every single person I interviewed for this book recalled a time when they sat in silence and didn't use their voice. So, let me ask you: When was the last time you stayed quiet? When was the last time you hesitated and sat in silence? When was the last time your True Inner Voice offered an answer to a question, and instead of opening your mouth, you remained mute?

SILENCE KILLS

My inability to use my voice took a life-threatening evil turn in 2011. As I detailed in Chapter 2, Tim and Jackie were skiing in the mountains. It was the first day in a very long time that I had the house to myself. I began to feel off and not well. I decided not to call anyone for help, as I didn't want to interrupt their day. I embraced staying quiet. The pain worsened, and I physically got sick. Still, I stayed quiet. I stayed quiet until my husband came home and rushed me to the hospital.

As I remember that moment, I want to smack myself upside the head. What was I thinking? I almost *died* because I didn't want to pick up the phone and use my voice. My inner chatter said I didn't want the attention. I didn't want to be a bother. I didn't want to interrupt the day of any of my friends.

I felt the fear and let it stop me in my tracks.

Several surgeries later, I wondered what the heck kind of example I was setting for my daughter. What would her life be like without a mother? What if she grew up to be exactly like me? Right then, I decided to be different. I would learn how to use my voice and be my own advocate. I would never let fear stop me in my tracks again. I am the example for my daughter. I must show her how to take care of herself.

Does this sound familiar—the fear part, if not the hospital part? Do you struggle to use your own voice? Do you hesitate? Do you ignore your inner voice and stay quiet? If so, you are not alone. Most people struggle. Some of the lucky ones feel the fear and use their voice anyway.

I am not one of those people. I felt the fear and stayed quiet. I had to learn how to use my voice. I had to change. I had to make a shift. Shifting is not an easy thing. In fact, of all the work I've done to shift and become my own advocate, learning to use my voice was the hardest. Yet, I did it! It can happen. Know that you can shift too. You can learn to use your voice. Keep reading.

HOW TO START

How do you un-silence your voice? How do you open

your mouth and share your words, your wisdom, and your knowledge? You start by choosing to not stay quiet. You feel the fear and do it anyway. You make a change.

YOU OPEN YOUR MOUTH AND LET YOUR WORDS BE HEARD.

I compare using my voice to running or swimming, both of which, when you're not experienced, are forms of torture in my world. When I asked my trainer, "How do I run faster?" she said, "You run faster." When I asked her, "How do I swim faster?" she said, "You swim faster. You just do it. You put forth the effort and go faster." In order to use your voice more, you make a conscious effort to use your voice.

Is it that simple? Yes. It honestly is that simple. Is it easy? No! As an introvert, the idea of using my voice was terrifying on so many levels. I had stayed quiet and comfortable for years. I had let my fear keep me silent. How do you make this critical shift? Where do you start?

Start by using your voice in a SAFE SPACE. Start by using your voice with a SAFE PERSON.

Who is your Safe Person? You are the only one who can answer. Here are some questions that may help.

What person in your life makes you feel safe? Who is the person that you trust? Who is the person you can interact with on a regular basis and be your true self? Who makes you feel secure? What name comes to mind? He or she is your Safe Person. My Safe Person is my husband, Tim. He is the one person who makes me feel whole, secure, loved, and needed. Take a moment and identify your one person.

Now that you have identified your Safe Person, let's get to work. First, let your Safe Person in on what you are about to do, which is participate in an experiment for six months. Fill him or her in as your partner and ask for his or her acceptance in your experiment. Say that you are working to create a new version of you. Say you will be using your voice, speaking up, and no longer staying silent in your conversations with this Safe Person. Explain that he or she is your Safe Person in this experiment. Ask him or her to allow you the space to change, shift, and use your voice.

Once your Safe Person agrees—and you know he or she will—you can start to have fun!

Your conversation with your Safe Person about this experiment lays the groundwork for you to start using you voice. Start right away. By identifying your Safe

Person and gaining permission to use your voice, you have created your Safe Space.

From here on in your everyday life, pay attention to your conversations in the same way you do with your inner voice and your Committee. In conversation, your brain works through solutions in your head and your True Inner Voice speaks to you. When you hear this voice, do you feel hesitant? Pause, pay attention, and recognize the hesitation. Say, "Thank you." Say, "I am in my Safe Space with my Safe Person. It's OK. I'm OK." Your Safe Person knows you are going to speak. Take in a deep breath of courage, exhale your fear, and speak. Open your mouth and share your thoughts, your ideas, your voice, your true self with your Safe Person. Use your voice. Feel the shift.

SELFISH OR IDEA SHARING?

At first, using your voice will feel uncomfortable. You might feel selfish. You might even feel awkward and unnatural. A hundred different thoughts will tell you why this doesn't feel right. In fact, you might feel like you are doing something wrong. That's your past chatting you up. That's your old programming. That's your Itty-Bitty Shitty Committee. What you need to know now is that your voice matters. Your opinions matter. You matter. You add value to all conversations, and the world wants to know what you think.

This shift is huge. My first conversation with Tim after I designated him as my Safe Person was in the car. We were heading out for dinner (the perks of having only one child—a sleepover with friend equals impromptu date night!), and Tim turned to me in his normal way and asked, "Where would you like to go for dinner?" My go-to response had always been that I didn't care, but now I was paying attention. I recognized my hesitation and heard my True Inner Voice speaking. Time to put this process to work. I closed my eyes, took a breath, and offered a suggestion. It was a Mexican restaurant, and that's not his favorite. He smiled and said, "OK. Let's go!" I smiled back. *Wait? Whaaaat? It was that easy?* There was a total dance party going on inside my head. *I did it! I put my thoughts, wants, desires, and needs first and used my voice!* My smile got so big you'd have thought I was the Cheshire Cat.

I remember feeling in that moment like I was putting my needs before his. I felt selfish. That's part of what made me uncomfortable to use my voice in the first place. That judgment was from my Itty-Bitty Shitty Committee.

In reality, I simply offered a suggestion for a type of food that appealed to me. I was sharing my wishes. It was up to him to agree or disagree. Using my voice wasn't self-ish. It was idea sharing.

All too often speaking our mind and using our voice are perceived as or misunderstood as being selfish. It is misunderstood that those in front of the room, on the stage, or at the microphone using their voice, speaking their mind, must have an agenda and are trying to sell something. It is misunderstood they are thinking only of themselves. In most cases, though, the people at the front of the room are in the same boat as you and I. They have an idea to share and fear using their voice and being misunderstood. Let me be clear. When you share your thoughts, your wishes, and your desires from a place of service with grace, you will NEVER be selfish as you use your voice.

Fast-forward six months. Tim and I were back in the car having the same conversation. He asked what I would like for dinner, and I responded with my favorite Mexican restaurant. *You know, those margaritas and queso are tasty!* This time, he said, "No, that doesn't sound good. What else do you want?" I made another suggestion. Again, he responded with a no. I offered a third dinner option and again he said no. Without hesitation, I looked at my Safe Person and said, "So I have given you several options that you don't like. It seems to me that you have something in mind. Why don't you tell me what you want to eat, and I will let you know if it sounds good?" (Insert sassy sarcastic tone here.) Without hesitation, I had used my voice, spoken my truth, and participated in our dinner plans for the night.

When it comes to my husband and food, I can honestly say that I now use my voice without hesitation. That was my first step (of many baby steps). I have grown more and more confident in using my voice. Soon after that dinner conversation, I felt comfortable enough to voice my thoughts in other life and business situations and conversations. I attended a Chamber leadership meeting where we talked about having a panel of speakers to present to our women's group on the topic of self-care. Who did I know who could talk on self-care? My True Inner Voice shouted, *ME! ME! ME!* Because I was paying attention, I felt the hesitation. I took a deep breath, inhaled courage, exhaled the fear, and used my voice. The idea was well received, and that was the first time I spoke about the power of using your voice.

Little by little, as you practice using your voice with

your Safe Person, your confidence grows. You feel less and less hesitation. You feel less and less fear. Your voice flows outward to all areas of your life, and you add value everywhere. You finally are empowered to use your voice with your entire family, in meetings, at work, and everywhere else you show up.

If I can do this, you can do this. One small shift, one small step, one small activity will eventually land you across the finish line, boldly using your voice.

ACTION STEPS
to Speak Your Truth

- Find your Safe Person.

- Inform your Safe Person about the six-month experiment and start immediately.

- Recognize the hesitation, inhale courage, exhale fear, and use your voice.

Chapter 7

REJECTION

THE PAIN

From as early as I can remember, I wanted to be a boy. It's not for reasons you might think. It's not a gender identity thing. It's an opportunity thing. In the Midwest where I grew up, the boys ruled the roost, generation after generation. Boys were to be seen and heard. Conversation after conversation was about the boys, what they were doing, what they were learning, whom they were dating, or where they were working. Boys got the attention, the praise, the encouragement, and even the adoration. Girls, on the other hand, were to be seen and NOT heard. At most of our family gatherings, the girls stayed in the kitchen preparing the food and doing the dishes. It didn't matter the number of family members at the table or the reason for the gathering, this was always the case. Girls were to serve.

It rubbed me wrong.

At times I tried to hang out with the boys, but it never worked. Inevitably, I would be told to go help my mother or find something else to do. I never really felt like I belonged.

Rejection takes various forms. You can be denied inclusion in a group. You can be denied participation in a sport. You can be denied a job. You can be denied a romantic relationship. You can be denied a loan. Rejection, regardless of its form, hurts. Rejection leaves scars. If we let it, rejection is integrated into our past and sets the tone for our future.

As a teenager, I talked on the phone for hours. I know, shocker! Let me set the stage for you. It was the 1980s, and technology was hugely inferior compared to today. In my home, we had only two telephones, and they were attached to walls. Literally. One was in my parents' bedroom, and we were not allowed to hang out there. The other was attached to the kitchen wall. If you wanted to take a "private" call in our house, you stretched the telephone cord around the corner of the kitchen wall past the dining room and sat in the living room corner. It was a funny sight. With three siblings in the house, there wasn't much opportunity to have a long (let alone, private) conversation. Also, voicemail and call waiting didn't exist yet. If you were on the phone when someone tried to call, the caller heard a "busy signal." If you were not home to answer the call, it might as well never have happened. Messages were taken by hand, and there was no caller ID. So, when you did time it right to talk on the phone, you were lucky and made do with the situation.

At the delicate age of fifteen, I was crushing on a boy, aka Dream Boat. He was older than I was, was so smart and funny, and he had the best smile. I am pretty sure Dream Boat didn't even know I existed. That didn't mean I couldn't talk about him with my friends, which I did— on the phone in one of my "private" calls. One evening, my father told me over dinner that a certain boy had called for me. *What? Really?* He said Dream Boat's name, and I was in shock. *Holy cow! Dream Boat knows who I am! He found out my number and called.* I immediately interrogated my father. "What did he say? What did he want? Am I to call him back?" My father just shrugged. "I don't know. I am not your secretary."

Holy cow! I was about to hyperventilate. After dinner, I hopped on the phone with my girlfriend and talked and talked and talked about THE call. What did he want? How could he get my number? *WOW! WOW! WOW!* This was so exciting.

The next day, I spent extra care in the morning to look nice. I fixed my hair. I fixed my makeup and even sprayed on a little of my mother's favorite perfume so I smelled nice. (Ssshhh ... don't tell her.) On the way to school, my heart was racing. I rode the bus with my neighbors and couldn't talk at all. My mind was in a whirl. *When would I see him? What would I say to him?* So much to think about. I was bursting with excitement that someone would like ME!

I hung around his locker between classes, just waiting for the opportunity to see him. I had this romantic story in my head. *We connect eyes. He walks up and says, "I've been looking all over for you."* Lunch time came, and I knew I would see him. I sat at the table with my friends but couldn't eat a thing. How could I? *My crush called ME! He called ME!!* My stomach was doing flips. The anticipation of a conversation with Dream Boat was too much.

I spotted him and stopped in my tracks. He didn't see me. Did I have the courage to walk over to him? *Yes ...*

yes! I walked his way and it happened. Our eyes met. We held a look for one ... two ... three seconds. My heart was holding a dance party. I smiled. Not just any smile, but a toothy, silly, ear-to-ear grin. He didn't smile. Odd. He looked away, but I kept walking toward him. My moment had arrived. I took a deep breath and stood there with all my teeth exposed. Another deep breath.

"I got your message," I said.

His face changed in an unexpected way. "What message?" he asked.

"You called yesterday."

His face contorted. His lips turned as if he had tasted something sour. He snorted, "I didn't call YOU! I wouldn't call YOU!"

Rejection. *Complete and utter rejection.*

I headed home after school to do my homework and prepare dinner for the family. My mind kept replaying the conversation with Dream Boat. That look of disgust! He was so mean. *How could I get this so wrong?*

When my parents got home from work, we sat down for dinner. We went around the table talking about our day, and I asked Dad about the message. I explained what happened and Dad busted into a belly laugh. A slap-my-ass-and-call-me-happy kind of laugh. Loud. Obnoxious.

Nearly choking on his food, he said it was a joke! The message. All of it. It was a joke! He had heard me talking about this boy, and he thought it would be funny to play a joke on me.

I was the joke.

Rejection sucks.

Moments like these leave a mark and define who we are deep down. Good or bad, they shape us. You can bet this moment was stored in my database, and it shaped me.

Rejection leaves scars. Scars that live on the inside deep in your soul. You can't see them, but, boy, can you feel them. The pain they carry shows up every time you feel you are being rejected. It stops you in your tracks. It makes you want to run and hide.

Most people have been rejected in a way that knocked them down. I share this story to let you know you are not alone. We all have been rejected, and that rejection has shaped us. My experience defined me. It created massive fear and unhinged my confidence. For years, I lived in fear of rejection. With the help of others, workshops, and books, I learned how to shift my understanding of rejection. I learned to shift my fear of rejection so that it no longer defines me. I did it. You can too.

THE LESSON

Know this: Rejection is all around you. You have been rejected multiple times already today, and you don't even know it. Rejection is a part of life, and it is healthy. Let's say you and I are sitting together on a plane to Cleveland, Ohio. (Don't judge—I love my hometown. It's a great place to be from.) You pull out a pack of chewing gum and offer me a stick. I say, "No, thank you." Right there is rejection. But how does that make you feel? Do you even care? Do you spend minutes or hours wondering why I said no? Or do you let it go? I'm guessing you let it go and don't give it a second thought.

You see, rejection is part of everyday life. It's no big deal most of the time, as it's all about choice. But rejection that ties into our emotions—now, that's another story. We do care. How much we care ties into how much emotion we feel for the subject. Let's say you offer a soda to your friend at home. He or she asks if you have Coke or Pepsi. Most people have a clear feeling and desire toward one of these sodas and a distaste for the other. They want Pepsi, and you only have Coke, so they decline. Chances are you won't worry whether you should change from Coke to Pepsi. Am I right?

Saying no or picking one item over another is a form of rejection. We say no and make choices all day long without a thought-charged debate in our head. Understand that all rejection is simply someone's choice. It is a decision they made based on their preferences, and it has little to do with you.

Suppose you are interviewing for a position at a firm, and you really want the job. You prepare, you show up, you interview, and you think you've got the job. You then learn they gave it to someone else. Rejection. This rejection has emotional ties, as you invested your effort, and your heart and soul, in this journey. Rejection like this, although uncomfortable and emotional, is not to be feared.

Fear can stop you from taking an interview in the first place. I invite you to shift your thinking. It's all about how you perceive the rejection. The interview itself was an opportunity. The interview itself was a form of acceptance. Others also applied and were rejected prior to your interview. The rejection is not saying no to you. Rather, it is saying yes to someone else. It was a choice. Shift your thinking. You are the Coke.

REJECTION HAS POWER WHEN YOU GIVE IT POWER. REJECTION HAS POWER WHEN YOU FEAR IT.

As if being an introvert weren't hard enough, I also suffered from low self-esteem and low self-confidence. That's a dangerous combination, especially when it came to rejection. I gave rejection so much power that I avoided it at all costs. I would bend over backward so that people would like me. My first husband decided he didn't want to be married anymore. He was not faithful, and he considered the marriage vows to be mere guidelines. We talked, and he suggested an open marriage. My True Inner Voice was screaming. That went against all my core values, but I didn't have the tools to listen and cope. My enormous fear of failure and a failed marriage made me consider the option for one hot second. Fortunately, my True Inner Voice kicked in, I packed my bags, and I moved out.

Here's something else I learned: Rejection has nothing to do with you. Rejection stems from the individual making the decision, and you are irrelevant in that equation. The rejection itself is about the person doing the rejecting. It's their decision. The rejection comes from their thoughts, beliefs, feelings, needs, and preferences, not from anything about you. Like the Pepsi/Coke choice, the outcome may impact you, but it has nothing to do with you. Plain and simple.

I interviewed about fifty people as I prepared to write this book. Every single person I interviewed is successful in their own way—lawyer, business owner, investor, teacher, etc. What they all had in common was their ability to face rejection as a challenge and not hold onto it like a curse. Rejection didn't derail them or hold them back. They learned from their experiences, and they grew. They embraced rejection. In fact, about half the people I interviewed had turned a rejection around and used it to move them forward. They perceived the rejection as an opportunity.

REJECTION HAS POWER WHEN YOU GIVE IT POWER. REJECTION LOSES POWER WHEN YOU SHIFT YOUR PERCEPTION.

There will be times in your life when rejection hurts. I am not going to lie about that. It will hurt. It might even feel as if it is ripping your heart out. It's the fear of it that stops us in our tracks. It's the fear that paralyzes us and our life energy. I hurt like hell when my first husband ended our marriage. I mean knock-me-to-my-knees hurt. Yet, I didn't let the fear stop me. Shortly after filing for divorce, I started dating my current husband. When one door closes, another one opens. Don't let the fear stop you from opening that door.

Rejection paves the way for growth and change. Rejection is about lessons. Rejection is about making choices. Shift your thinking to see rejection as something to embrace, an opportunity, a lesson. When you make that shift, your fear fades and you begin to grow.

As a business owner, I had to learn to be good at sales. I used to say I hated the idea of sales and hated selling. Then I realized that we are all selling every single day. When I worked as a paralegal, I was selling the firm. When my daughter's school held a raffle, I was selling raffle tickets. I learned to get comfortable with discomfort and to accept rejection. I learned to hear no and remember that it was not personal. I learned to let go of my emotional baggage from past rejections and to think Coke or Pepsi.

Write down this phrase and post it around your home or in your work space:

Some will. Some won't. So what? Someone's waiting.

For those of you with a business mindset, I offer up a game to play as you make your sales calls, connect with your contacts and referrals, and ask for the business. I've used this tool for years, and it has allowed me to embrace rejection. I call the game, The 100 No's Challenge. It's a grid with one-hundred boxes. In each box is the word *No*. Rewards are located in the *No* boxes. Find a free copy of this challenge on my website, www. sharingtheshine.com, under the Mantras and Mindset tab. Use it. As you make your calls, your contacts, your offerings, keep track of the No's. When you hit a box with a reward, celebrate. Celebrate the rejection. Celebrate the No.

This shifts how you perceive the no you hear from your prospect. You celebrate the no. Some will. Some won't. So what? Someone's waiting.

When it comes to matters of the heart and the Dream Boats out there, rejection will happen. Some will. Some won't. So what? Someone's waiting.

As a happily married woman with a successful business in health and wellness, I work every day on facing my fear of the no. I learned to be comfortable with being uncomfortable and to face my fear of rejection. I am grateful for the lessons that come from rejections, and I move forward.

Some will. Some won't. So what? Someone's waiting.

ACTION STEPS
to Relieve Rejection

- Remember, it's only a choice. It's not about you. It's Coke or Pepsi.

- Take the 100 No's Challenge. Download from sharingtheshine.com under Mantras and Mindset.

Chapter 8

GRATITUDE

APPRECIATE TODAY

The harsh reality is there are no promises or guarantees in life. Tomorrow is not a given. Today is a gift. Every opportunity, every challenge, every daily lesson, whether you worked for it or not, is a gift. Whether you are a baby needing milk, a teenager needing a car, a college graduate needing a job, a couple needing a baby, a grandparent needing medical treatment, there is nothing in this world that is a given. Nothing is certain.

As someone who has faced the possibility of no tomorrow, I know this harsh reality. Every day is a precious gift and one to be embraced, cherished, and counted as a blessing.

We all have suffered in one way or another. Each one of us has struggled. Some have hit rock bottom. Hitting rock bottom offers good points along with the bad. At rock bottom, you have a decision to make: stay in the craziness and possibly die, or change, make shifts, and fight back.

I hit my rock bottom in 2011 after nearly losing my life because of my fear of speaking up. You don't need to experience a hospital visit before you make a change. Learn from my lesson and let it sink into your soul. Know that tomorrow is not a given, yesterday is gone, and today—this day—is a gift.

In my rock bottom, I faced surgery after surgery after surgery in a very short period of time. Only one of those surgeries was life threatening. When I faced the possibility that tomorrow might not come, when my doctors told me I was lucky to be alive, when I worried I might never snuggle the love of my life again or get to watch my child grow and mature, I looked long and hard at my life. I became grateful. Really grateful.

TOMORROW IS NOT A GIVEN.
YESTERDAY IS GONE. TODAY—
THIS DAY—IS A GIFT.

I have always been an optimist. I get that from my mother. I do see the glass as half full, no matter the circumstances. My first surgery was on my foot. (That one was planned.) My second surgery was for an ectopic pregnancy. That one almost killed me. And yet, even in the face of a near-death experience, the only thing that stayed in my mind was that I had gotten pregnant. *I was pregnant!* It gave me hope. I was grateful.

Fast-forward five years to a normal day in my life as a wife, mother, and business owner. In the middle of the night I felt a shooting pain in my calf. The bottom half of my leg was hard as a rock. I had gone running that morning, and I had networked in my "big girl" heels that day, so I thought I was having my first charley horse. I carefully rolled out of bed so as not to wake my husband, and I rubbed my leg with my foam roller. The pain was excruciating, but after a while, I felt some relief.

The next day, my leg was sore, but I wasn't in pain. *Fabulous! My cup is half full.* In the late afternoon, I noticed a pain in my right back rib. I had felt this once before, when I was so stressed that my ribs popped out of place. (Did you know they could do that?) I figured it was time for a massage, and I made an appointment to nip this in the bud. Twenty-four hours later, when I was working from home, the pain in my back grew from annoying to knocking me to my knees. I could not breathe.

This time, I didn't hesitate to ask for help. I called the doctor and came up with a plan. I called my neighbor, used my voice, and asked for a ride. My neighbor took me to the nearest ER. The doctors told me I had blood clots covering both of my lungs. Doctor after doctor told me I was lucky to be alive. The doctors said my healthy lifestyle had saved my life.

Lucky to be alive.

Lucky to be alive.

Not once but twice, I have faced a day when I might not see tomorrow. Through each of my crises, I grew in strength and gratitude. Now I walk through each day knowing tomorrow is not a given, yesterday is gone, and today—this day—is a gift.

Truth be told, even the happiest people on earth have an occasional bad day. They get cranky. They have moments when they want to smack someone upside the head. We're all human. We all have emotions and hopes that can be crushed in one sweeping instant. It's OK if you are not an optimist. It's OK if you do not wear rose-colored glasses. I invite you to walk through life with gratitude. With gratitude comes joy, happiness, peace, and the ability to show up as your authentic self.

JOURNALING

What we think about we bring about. You've probably heard this before. Whole libraries of lessons and books support this concept, and it all comes down to the power of positive thinking. You cannot be grateful when you are angry, and you cannot be angry when you are grateful. Thus, if we wish to reduce anger, we need to shift into gratitude.

How do we show up as grateful? We can start with gratitude for our desk and our car and our family. But we have to go deeper. We have to get our emotions involved. We have to communicate with our True Inner Self. We have to spend time being quiet. Keeping a journal helps.

I CANNOT OVEREMPHASIZE THE
POWER OF JOURNALING.

I won't bore you with the scientific details; just know

that there is scientific support for the effectiveness of journaling. At first, I was a bit of a skeptic. Yeah, this optimistic, happy introvert didn't really like the idea of journaling for gratitude. But when I was in therapy for my divorce, I learned to vent on paper. It allowed me to have a voice and work through my struggles. Based on that experience and having studied the science, I gave it a shot.

Gratitude journaling takes many forms. Pick out what's right for you and your lifestyle. You can journal any time of day, in any place, and with anything—that is, it doesn't have to be a formal journal. A spiral-bound notebook or legal pad works for a journal. You can use pen or pencil. You can even use your computer or tablet (but see Julia Cameron's advice in *The Artist's Way* about the benefit of writing with pen and paper instead of on a computer). You need only time and space to get quiet, something to write on, and something to write with.

Here's a popular technique many journalers practice. Keep a gratitude journal next to your bed. Get ready for bed, and before you turn out the light, grab your journal and become quiet. Take some deep breaths to clear your mind. Talk to your True Inner Self and ask, "What am I grateful for today?" Write down at least three things that come to mind that you are grateful for that day. Follow that up with asking yourself, "Why am I grateful for this today?" and write the reasons. For example, you can write, "I am grateful for my car. Because of my car, I was able to get to my appointments on time today without stress or worry." Or, "I am grateful for my dog. Because of my dog, I was able to forget my to-do list for a few moments and play like a child outside in the sun." Notice how including your *why*—"without stress or worry," "play like a child in the sun"—brings you to the good energy and feelings.

Journal at the time that works best for you. Some people journal first thing in the morning or right after meditation. Some journal at two o'clock every afternoon. Find a time that works for you, your schedule, and your presence of mind. It's important to be in a quiet space with no distractions and to calm your mind. Your quiet mind opens you to feeling and expressing gratitude.

MY STORY

You can imagine I was a little cranky after all my surgeries. My body hurt and my energy level was low. I couldn't do things I had been accustomed to doing. My recovery was long and annoying, and I was impatient.

I vented most of my anger at my husband—my Safe Person. I can be my true self with him, and I was unhappy. Things that would normally roll off my back or make me laugh now made me yell or cry. I remember hearing myself yell and wondering, *who is this person?* Remember, I am the happy introvert. Being cranky isn't my norm. Because I was out of my norm, I was cranky for being cranky. I decided to take this journaling thing to the next level.

I created a gratitude journal that would focus on my husband. My plan was to journal every day for a year and then present him with the journal as a gift for his birthday. In the end, this gratitude journal would be 365 reasons I appreciate him.

Because I was cranky in the beginning, it took some time for me to get into an emotional space of gratitude. I realized that, being as cranky as I was, journaling next to him in bed wasn't going to work for me. Tim has one of those internal switches: when he wants to sleep, he just closes his eyes. It takes me a while to get to sleep, so trying to be grateful when I was full of jealousy didn't work. He needed to be out of my sight, and I needed to have my own space. I selected a time midday when no one was around. I kept my journal near my desk. Every day, I would spend five or ten minutes on the journal. I would get quiet and think about the day before. What had Tim done that made me smile? What had he done to show his love? What had he done that didn't make me want to smack him upside the head? I started small with my journaling journey.

By the second month, I felt a shift in my energy and my anger. My conversations and my attentiveness with him shifted. I felt a shift to deeper love.

What we think about we bring about. When I began, I recognized Tim's love and support and the character-istics that are his true self, but I wasn't really feeling the gratitude. After journaling over time, I began to feel all of it. With the feeling of gratitude every day, I started no-ticing more and more things he did or said that made me grateful. Our love grew richer that year. My heart grew that year. I am human, and I still get cranky at times, but in spite of that, I feel truly grateful for Tim.

It's one thing to *say* we are grateful. It's entirely differ-ent to *feel* it and *mean* it.

Concurrently with my 2016 health crisis, my mother was dealing with her own health issues. We lived states apart, and we would talk on the phone several times a week and commiserate about how much fun it was to see the doctor all the time (*not*). My weekly doctor trips were to get iron infused in my blood. My mother's doctor trips were to remove the iron from her blood. We laughed about this and thought we made quite the pair. It would save us a lot of trouble if she could simply give her iron to me!

My mother's iron issues worsened, as did other issues with her health and wellness. She had negative reactions to various medications. Medication for one problem would create another, over and over in a chain reaction. Months later, my sister called to say that Mom was in the hospital. I flew out to Ohio to cheer her on to a speedy recovery. But days and weeks passed, and her body refused to recover. With each passing day, I saw my mother melting before me. Her energy and vibrancy drained daily, and it wasn't long before I could see she had given up the will to live. All the time she was in the hospital, she kept telling us how sorry she was to be so much trouble.

Mom hadn't opened her eyes for days. On a very cold day in February, we learned her kidneys had stopped functioning. Her every breath was a struggle. The doctors said it wouldn't be long. The family gathered by her bedside and talked to her about joining her sister and brother in heaven. I sat in the bed with her, her hand in my hand. Those beautiful hands had once combed my hair, wiped my tears, cared for my boo-boos, and on occasion cracked my backside for being sassy. Now they were still, lifeless, and so small.

I watched my mother take her last breath and told her I loved her. It was surreal, exceptionally difficult to watch, and not peaceful. Her last breaths were a struggle. She would open her mouth and fight and fight to take in any air. In less than a minute, her lungs stopped trying, and her body said, *no more.* She was still.

Tomorrow is not a given, yesterday is gone, and today—this day—is a gift.

Watching the life leave my mother was a blessing and a curse. It was one of the hardest moments of my life, yet it brought me to the hard truth. Each day is a blessing and a gift. I am grateful for the time I had in my past and for the time I have today.

I have devoted a good deal of space to my experiences in this chapter for a reason. My experiences are extraordinary and not normal. My goal in sharing my struggles, my fears, and my lows is to make you aware enough of the lessons I learned that you can make a shift. I invite you to hear my lessons and choose to use your voice, with my support and my gratitude.

My first thought on waking each day is, *Thank you, God, for the gift of this day*. I thank the entire universe for all that I have on each day. And now, I also thank my mother and ask her to watch over me as I take on the day.

Find ways to be grateful every day and write in your gratitude journal. Open your mind and your heart to the feeling of gratitude. Remember, we cannot be grateful and angry at the same time. What we think about we bring about, so take it a step further. Place notes around your home, in your office, in your car, in the kitchen, maybe even on the back of your phone to remind you to feel grateful.

Today is a gift; everything that happens today is a gift, and it's worthy of your gratitude.

What are you grateful for right now? Forget about what's missing. Forget about comparing yourself to others or pushing for the next best thing. Let that go. Focus on what's going right in your world. Focus on what brings you joy. Focus on all the love in your life.

Gratitude comes from focusing on what you have, not on what you lack. It comes from cherishing what is, not struggling over what's missing. Enjoyment for what we have increases our happiness. Shift your thoughts and express your gratitude for all that's in your life today and watch your authentic self shine. That is your path to happiness.

ACTION STEPS
to Be in Gratitude

- Begin a gratitude journal.
- Be grateful every single day.

Chapter 9

CONFIDENCE

THE SIMPLE TRUTH

Confidence–as defined by the online dictionary *merriam-webster.com*—has several complex definitions: "a feeling or consciousness of one's powers or of reliance on one's circumstances; faith or belief that one will act in a right, proper, or effective way; the quality or state of being certain."

Here is the simple truth about confidence: Confidence is not a trait you are born with; it is something you develop. If you are not a confident person, you can absolutely become one. And if you are a confident person, you can absolutely un-become one. Our circumstances, successes, failures, peers, and self-talk all play into our level of confidence.

Confidence is a state of mind and requires feedback and assurances. You receive assurance when you accomplish a task, experience success, overcome a failure, receive positive feedback, or receive support from your peers and authority figures. Your daily positive self-talk has a huge impact on your confidence level. These assurances bolster your belief in your own abilities. Consider Olympic athletes. When they are competing, we see them at their peak. We do not see all that it took for them to get to that level. They trained, they received coaching, they practiced, they trained some more, they logged long hours of exertion, and they shed blood, sweat, and tears. They worked hard. Confidence is like an Olympic sport. It requires training, attention, and work.

Here are some phrases to incorporate into your training:

Fake it till you make it.

Practice makes perfect.

What you think about you bring about.

FAKE IT TILL YOU MAKE IT

How do you fake confidence? Posture! There are two aspects of posture to consider: physical and mental. Both tell a story of confidence or the lack thereof. What do your postures say about you?

It is simple to shift physical posture into an appearance of confidence. Our mothers were right to tell us to stand tall with chin up and shoulders back. Whether they realized it or not, they were teaching us to create an appearance of confidence. Your posture tells a story. Do you pay attention to how you are sitting? Standing? Entering a room? I invite you to pay attention to your posture, especially when you are in a situation where you want to look and feel more confident.

Looking confident is so easy that anyone can do it. Before you enter a room or attend a meeting, or as you sit at a table or desk, take a large, deep breath. Allow the air to fill your entire chest and stretch the upper half of your body toward the sky. Let your head reach up, lift your chin slightly, and pull your shoulders back to open your chest. Fill your lungs to capacity. If you are standing, you can even go into the superhero stance by spreading your feet shoulder-width apart and placing your hands on your hips. Think confidence. Think superpowers.

At the top of your inhale, hold your breath for a count of three and release without shifting your head, shoulders, or back. Maintain your posture. This little exercise makes you taller, thinner, and more confident. Boom!

To take this exercise a little further, stand in the superhero pose (think Wonder Woman) for a few minutes. Hold the posture, inhale confidence, and release your fear on the exhale.

There are two reasons why shifting your physical posture builds confidence. First, it literally shifts you; holding the posture triggers a chemical shift in your brain and body, and you feel more confident. Second, it shifts the others in the room. When you physically stand or sit in a confident pose, others notice your confidence and treat you accordingly. It's the best of both worlds.

55% OF OUR COMMUNICATION IS POSTURE AND BODY LANGUAGE.

According to Professor Albert Mehrabian, our verbal language makes up only about 7 percent of our message. Our tone and voice make up 38 percent, and the remaining 55 percent of our communication is nonverbal—it's our posture and body language. As we pay attention and strike a pose of confidence, we affect how others see us. When you aren't feeling confident, fake it by holding a confident physical posture and notice the result.

The second aspect of posture is mental and affects how we say what we say. As Mehrabian said, 38 percent of communication is tone and voice. Have you ever noticed that when someone asks a question, their inflection goes up at the end? This also happens when we say something and are not sure of its validity or truth. Our vocal inflection rises at the end as if we are asking ourselves a question. And when that happens, we don't sound like we know what we're talking about. We don't sound confident.

In your conversations, do you know what you're talking about? Are you informed? Educated? Have you done your research? Do you have the knowledge and authority to speak on the message you share? Or are you full of it? If you wish to speak with a confident posture, do your research. Know your subject matter.

Let's say you are shopping for a new car. You head to the dealer and a salesperson offers to assist you. You ask questions about performance, fuel economy, and safety. The salesperson doesn't know any of the answers and keeps referring to the sticker. Is he displaying a posture of confidence? No. If, instead, he answers all your questions and shares useful additional information, how would you perceive him? You would see him as confident.

Here's a tip about posture as a businessperson. Posture doesn't require PERSONAL knowledge or experience with a product. There are plenty of men who work in the makeup industry. Do these men wear makeup? Some, maybe, but most have never worn eyeliner or lipstick. Their posture and confidence come from having done the research. They know about product testing. They know about product experiences. They can offer real facts, real statistics, real information on the subject. Their knowledge gives them a confident posture.

MY STORY

I have been a business owner for years. When I first started my business, I joined various networking groups to grow my business. In these meetings, people were asked to give a thirty-second "commercial" that summarized who they were and how the people in the room could help them grow their business. I had never done that before, and my posture reflected that. Not only did I not know what to say, I also couldn't keep my voice from shaking. I sounded scared to death the entire time.

I did my research. I talked with other members of the group and learned how a good thirty-second commercial should sound. I wrote mine down so I could refer to it and not leave anything out. It took me about a year before I felt comfortable enough to just think about what I wanted to say and not have to write down every word. Eventually, I improved my posture, and my commercials brought me business.

PRACTICE MAKES PERFECT

You may have the best commercial in the world, but if you cannot deliver it without stuttering or throwing in nervous *ums* and *uhs*, you won't posture confidence. Here's where practice comes into play. Just like athletes practice their sport to build muscles, stamina, endurance, and skill, you must practice giving your talk in order to build your confidence until it becomes second nature. Rehearse your talk in front of a mirror, hold a conversation with your reflection, and do it over and over again. Watch your facial expressions as you speak. Your facial expressions, how you tilt your head, how you use your hands, and your tone of voice are all part of a confident posture.

Have you seen this scene in a movie? The actor stands in front of the mirror preparing for a speech, a talk, a date, a conversation, a request, a proposal, a business transaction, and he practices his talk. He looks at himself in the mirror and repeats his talk until it sounds right. Practice makes perfect.

If you struggle with confidence, know this. In writing this book, I interviewed a number of business owners, men and women who are leaders in their community. I asked each one about their confidence level and if they felt confidence was part of their nature. Not one individual I interviewed felt they were born with confidence. Each one had to learn it or develop it in some way.

In the early days of my networking and growing my business, I used these tools. I researched my product and how I served, I practiced how I spoke and networked, and I showed up to each meeting standing tall, chin up, chest open and shoulders back. I faked it until I made it. Over time, others could see the shift. They saw my confidence build. They saw my posture.

I still use these techniques whenever I am networking, hanging with family and friends, or participating in a school meeting. These techniques are my tools to pause my introverted nature and show up and shine. They give me great posture. They enhance my confidence.

Remember, we make our own confidence. Confidence is a shift in skills and posture. Be your own superhero. You can do this!

ACTION STEPS
to Enhance Confidence

- Stand in superhero (Wonder Woman) pose or sit, take a deep breath, lift your chin, open your chest and shoulders back.

- Pay attention to your body language.

- Practice, practice, practice.

Chapter 10

LEAD, FOLLOW, OR GET OUT OF THE WAY

LEADER OR FOLLOWER

I was a leader trapped in a follower's mind. Although following others my whole life never felt natural, it was the easier path. Following the crowd led me to make poor choices and ultimately led to the medical crisis that nearly cost me my life. Who needs that? No one. Even as I learned to step into my authentic self, listen for my True Inner Voice, use my voice, and surround myself with like-minded people, I still struggled to find focus and value.

Grown-ups used to ask me what I wanted to be when I grew up. To this day, I recall my first answer to that question. I was four years old, and my mother had brought my sister home from the hospital. She was so little and she smelled so good. She looked like a miracle to me. A gift. My answer to that question was simple. I wanted to be a mom.

The older I got, the more I realized that being a mom and having a career are not mutually exclusive. I have always wanted to help people, and I believed that being an attorney could help me do that and make a good living. I told my grandmother that when I made my first million dollars, I would pay off her home. The look on her face still warms my heart. She believed in me. She probably giggled at me too, but she told me I could do anything.

Fast-forward through my education and placement in a law firm after graduation. I began working in my dream profession supporting attorneys and other staff. As a paralegal I gained a deeper understanding of the law firm culture. The hours were long, there was tons of work, and in my twisted mind it was mostly fun. By my third year, another reality hit me. Being a lawyer, a good lawyer, would interfere with my dream of being a mother. At least, it would interfere with being the kind of mother I wanted to be.

So, I let it go. I gave up being an attorney to be a mother.

Here's my point: I had one dream; I had one serious goal. In every other area of my life, I played follow the leader, or I got out of the way. Little in my life was about me. I grew up in the supporting role of taking care of others, and that led me down an unhealthy path. Once I tuned into my True Inner Voice, identified my core values, and claimed ownership of my vision, I became the leader of my life.

When you listen to your inner voice and speak it out, you are equipped to lead in the face of fear and rejection. You have the tools to make decisions, to dream, to craft goals and plans that align with your core values.

A GOAL PLUS A VISION EQUALS A ROAD MAP TO LIVING A TRULY AUTHENTIC AND FULFILLED LIFE.

Your action steps toward your goals set a powerful example. You become a leader. You become your own advocate. When you honor your vision, you set boundaries, you create focus, and you powerfully embrace your true self.

A variety of professionals and experts have helped me shift into my own advocacy. I learned that getting clear on my core values and having a clear vision of how I want my life to look gave me permission to stand up for my true self, create boundaries, and honor those core values.

TUNE INTO YOUR CORE VALUES

Getting in touch with your core values is the first step. From there, you can create the vision statement for your life. Your life vision is a written statement of your goals in five areas—home life, spiritual life, physical life, work life, and financial life. Your vision speaks your truth, and it becomes the mantra for your morning meditation. Listen to your vision statement daily. Allow your conscious mind and subconscious mind to come together with one purpose: your vision.

IT'S TIME TO GET CLEAR AND THINK BIG.

Let's start with the end in mind. What would you like to see in three years? What do you look like? How old are you? Where do you live? What relationships are important and satisfying for you? How do you show up? How do you feel? What do you say to yourself? How do you handle challenges? Think about what you REALLY want.

Think about the activities, conversations, attitudes, feelings, and mindset (minus criminal activities, ha ha ha) you would enjoy if nothing were stopping you. Think end game. Close your eyes and see yourself three years from now going through your new normal day, with normal interactions, normal everything. Relish the picture for several minutes. Your vision will speak your dreams, your goals, and your truths.

Write your vision in quick lists. Don't spend too much time on it. Just let your thoughts, feelings, and goals take the reins.

Now that you know your three-year end game, let's think about how to get there. This will be your vision statement for today! As we address each of the categories below, break your three-year goal into action steps for today.

Home Life

This means something different for every person. For our purpose, we include not only your personal family or those living under your roof (spouse, children, pets) but also your extended family (parents, in-laws, grandchildren, siblings, cousins, etc.), your lover, your friends, and your close relationships. With whom do you interact every day? Those relationships and interactions make up

Home Life.

This category covers love, family, friendships, and relationships. What is your ideal household? What are your ideal relationships? How do you show up?

Spiritual Life

Do you believe in the energy around us, God, karma, or something else? Most of us acknowledge there is something bigger, a power bigger than we are that directs, guides, and helps us to live a life that is authentic and true to our core. What does that mean to you? Do you pray? Meditate? Get quiet? Journal? What actions or activities do you do that allow you to get in touch with your True Inner Voice, your authentic self? How do you want it to look, feel, and be? Do you need more? Do you want something simpler?

Giving and taking create balance. In your spiritual life, how do you serve and give back to those around you? How do you show up to give? Do you receive with grace?

Physical Life

What is your vision of the in-shape, healthy, strong, energetic, oh-so-kick-butt version of you? How does it feel to be that version? What do you do? What food do you eat? How often do you work out or move? What action steps are you doing daily, weekly, or monthly to achieve or maintain your goal? How does the perfect physical version of you show up?

Work Life

In a perfect world, what is your dream job? How do you serve? Whom do you serve? How do you show up? What are your skills, activities, and accomplishments in this dream job? How do you feel? Are you living it now? If not, what needs to shift in order to live it now? If you are living it now, what will make it better or more consistent? Do you strive for a promotion or have an income goal? What steps can you take to hit your goals?

Financial Life

In a perfect world, what do your finances look like? Do you make enough money? A butt-load of money? Do you save wisely? Do you own your home? Are you saving for your children? Will you sit pretty in retirement? Do you spend money wisely? How do you feel about your financial situation today? How do you want to feel? What actions will you take to feel secure with your finances?

Write Your Story

Once you have your vision for each area, write a story. Speak the story as if it is happening today. Tell how you begin and end every day. Describe your daily actions that lead you to your goals. Express how you feel as you do these things. Tell YOUR story as if you are the greatest thing to walk this earth and know that you will have it all.

Once your life vision is written, record it with inspirational music in the background. Listen to it first thing every morning to set the tone for your day. Hearing your story daily will bolster your commitment to yourself—how you show up in your home life, your spiritual life, your physical life, your work life, and your financial life. Listening daily inspires shifts and changes. Speaking your truth and your vision makes you well-equipped to handle the challenges that face you each day.

As you accomplish your goals and as life changes occur, craft your next-level vision and rerecord it.

ACTION STEPS
for Your Living Vision

- Get a tablet of paper and a pen or pencil.

- Write your three-year goals for home life, spiritual life, physical life, work life, and financial life.

- List the action steps you will take in the next three months, six months, and one year to accomplish your goals.

- Record your life vision story and listen to it daily.

Chapter 11

PROGRESS, NOT PERFECTION

MY STORY

When I was approaching my fortieth birthday, I couldn't help but contemplate my life over the preceding decade. I still scratch my head over the roller coaster ride and the number of changes I made in such a short period of time. I got divorced, bought a horse, bought a house then another, re-married, had a baby, and landed a new job. Whew! It was awesome to experience changing from being unhappy A LOT to being happy A LOT! Recovering from childbirth and two years of infertility treatments before that, I started to run with a friend and coworker. Her child's school run was my first taste. Next thing you know, we signed up to do the Race for the Cure. At that point, I can honestly say I did not love running, but I loved what it did for my body.

One evening, I received an email about an event called Tri for the Cure. *Tri? Interesting. What is that?* I did a little research and pondered if it was a smart option for me or even doable. Turns out "Tri" means three challenges in one event: swimming, biking, and running. This event was called a "sprint tri," so it was *only* (hear my sarcasm) a half-mile swim, an eleven-mile bike ride, and a 5K run. I had already successfully accomplished several 5Ks and had been biking with my husband. I just needed to learn to swim. (Side note: Although I had lived nearly forty years on the planet, I never really learned how to swim. I could tread water and dog paddle—that was it.) I emailed my friend. We had never talked about swimming before. I was curious to know her thoughts. Her return email the next day confirmed her registration. *Wait. WHAT? I said, "What do you think?"* Not, *"Let's do this!"* Turns out, she was in heavy work mode. She had spent half the night preparing for a big case. She had worked until nearly dawn and was loaded with caffeine when she read my email. She thought it sounded good, immediately registered for the event, and that was that.

Be careful what you ask for—you might get it.

I grew up with two parents who feared the water. My father loved the idea of fishing on a boat on top of the water, and my mother enjoyed being near the water but never in it. So, no surprise that their daughter never learned how to swim and was scared to put her face in the water. I looked at the event description again. The body of water would not be a swimming pool. It was an OPEN-WATER swim. (Insert curse word here.) I had never been in open water before. My feet would not be touching the bottom of the pool. Or lake. Or whatever. I would have no floor and no safety net. (Another curse word.) My heart races now, just remembering how I felt even thinking about being in an open-water swim with hundreds of other women for the first time ever.

First things first. Between anxiety attacks, I called my gym and asked about swimming lessons. Believe it or not, they had someone who could teach an adult like me to swim across the pool without touching bottom. Score! It was early in the year, and we had about six months to train. For the first time, I thought I might actually live through this.

I had my plan of attack. I would do swim lessons, I would bike with my husband, and I would run outside or on my treadmill, depending on the weather. Spring approached and I was gaining confidence in the pool. I could swim a half-mile without touching the floor of the pool. I was amazed how far I could go. Still, open water terrified me. As luck would have it (doh!), my neighborhood offered open-water swimming at the lake on weekends. I could test-drive an open-water swim. I did some research on how to not die in open water. (Yes, the Internet offers information about that!) One suggestion was to swim in a wet suit, as it is buoyant and will actually help you float. *Holy cow! Something that could help me float.* I loved the idea. I headed to the store.

Buying a wet suit is easy. Trying one on is not. I grabbed several suits from the rack and headed into the dressing room, wondering if there was a system to trying them on. I explained my inexperience to a worker in the store and asked for suggestions. He stopped laughing after he realized I was serious and gave me a few simple tips. Imagine cramming every inch of your body and every roll of fat into a suit that sticks to your skin and is ten sizes too small. It wasn't pleasant. Within fifteen minutes I was sweating profusely and needed to stick my head out of the dressing room for air. I think I lost ten pounds just wrestling with the suit. And if that's not funny enough, the suit didn't fit. It was too big. Finally, the third suit I tried on was acceptable to the sales team, who were now cracking open a few beers and laughing at the ordeal.

I went home excited to do my first open-water swim the next morning. Did you know that in the back of a wet suit, there is a place to put your name and contact information? I smiled at my husband and said, "How smart is that? It's a great way to identify the body! Woo-hoo!"

The next morning, I rose early and headed to the lake at the center of my neighborhood. It was a beautiful summer morning with a chill in the air. I smiled nervously at my friend at the launching site. She had had a similar experience with the wet suit, and we couldn't help but laugh as we slapped and squeezed our bodies into our suits. The water felt lusciously cool after the putting-on-the-suit workout. A handful of people watched us crazy swimmers walk to the lake, making sure we were all safe. I felt better knowing that people were paying attention to who was going out. They would take attendance as people returned.

When I reached the place where my feet could no longer touch ground, I tested the suit for floatability. My heart raced as I faced the reality that I might go down and not come up. My mind raced. *I can do this. I can do this.* I watched swimmer after swimmer head out to the course. They made it look so easy. *I can do this. I can do this.* I took a deep breath and let myself go to test the suit. I didn't tread water or try to swim. I simply let go. And get this—I floated! The suit worked. My insides did a happy dance. I was ready to tackle the course.

It took me a while, but I did it. I completed the half-mile swim in open water! I wasn't fast, and I was terrified of the creatures moving around my feet. I was comforted to know the wet suit would save me from all the little swimmy things if I panicked. I challenged myself to another three or four open-water swims in my neighborhood before the big event.

THE BIG EVENT

On event day, I loaded up my gear and headed to the staging area. Space had been designated for us to keep our bikes, towels, snacks, and gear. The game plan after each event was to come back to our section, change gear, and take off. I was all set and ready for the swim about thirty minutes before we needed to go the starting gate. Then I had to go potty.

An unfortunate reality. The thought of trying to peel my body out of a wet suit and stuff it back in while inside a porta potty was unattractive. I spoke with other athletes and learned a common trick: at the end of your last leg of the swim, go potty in the open water. I was certain they were lying to me, but the more athletes I talked to, the more it was confirmed. Well, there ya go.

All the athletes lined up according to age. We were stacked like horses being led into a pen. Wave after wave of swimmers were released to the water. I entered the water, and it was very cold. My heart raced waiting for the starting gun to go off. And then, BANG! The athletes took off. I hung out in the back, as my goal was to survive this task, not to set any records. I entered the water slowly and paid attention to my breathing. *One stroke at a time. One stroke at a time.* That's all I needed to focus on. In less than thirty minutes, I would complete this stage and walk out of the water and onto the dock. Back on the dock, my heart still raced. This time, though, I was cheering inside and out. Not only had I just survived in open water, but I had also completed the half-mile swim. I felt like Rocky the boxer when he ran up the stairs with his hands up in the air. He was the picture of victory, and I felt victorious. The remaining stages would be easy compared to this.

As I had faced what I thought was an impossible challenge that could end in death, I had taken small steps each day and each week on the path to complete it. Each day I had made progress and gained skill and confidence in the water.

It's about progress, not perfection.

How can we apply this same system to every area of life? Whether you are a spouse, a parent, a business owner, student, whatever, you work on tasks and challenges every day. Think about how you measure yourself and the tasks in your life. Are you making progress? Are you moving toward your end goal?

Make progress, not perfection.

What is perfection anyway? According to merriam-webster.com, "perfection" means: "the quality or state of being perfect: such as freedom from fault or defect (flawlessness), maturity, the quality or state of being saintly; an exemplification of supreme excellence; an unsurpassable degree of accuracy and excellence."

Freedom from fault or defect. Really? What human out there is free from fault? Free from defect? When it comes to us humans, is being perfect a realistic expectation? By Webster's definition, can we call even one human perfect? That's a big ol' *NO*! Humans are beautifully imperfect.

Beautifully different. Our differences and imperfections distinguish us from others and allow us to be our true selves. By definition, no human is perfect. So why do we strive for perfection?

COME TO TERMS AND BE FREE

Achieving perfection is unrealistic. Pursuit of it will never end in satisfaction.

BEING PERFECT IS NOT AN OPTION. LET IT GO.

When we let go of the demand for perfection, we are free to focus on progress.

Progress is the movement, whether big or small, toward your goals. What movement will help you reach your goals? I invite you, whether your goal is physical, financial, or even romantic, to focus on the steps to take and not on perfect results. Celebrate your action items and your progress. To learn to swim, I had to focus on small actions that made me a swimmer. I focused on my breathing; I focused on doing a lap without choking on water; I celebrated. Each step, each action, each swim resulted in progress and improvement. In the end, I celebrated my progress. And it is my progress that made me a successful triathlete.

To move forward with life and love, with family and community, and with business, focus on the steps. Make it about the progress and let go of the perfection.

ACTION STEPS
for Progress

- Let go of perfection.
- Celebrate progress.
- Celebrate often!

Chapter 12

BE BRAVE

COURAGE

John Wayne said, "Courage is being scared to death, but saddling up anyway."

Are you brave? Do you have courage? Young children have little fear. They run, they jump, they do "stupid" things because they don't know enough to be afraid. With age comes the "wisdom" to be afraid.

When you were old enough to walk and talk, your parents probably taught you about stranger danger. "Don't talk to strangers." In fact, you might have been taught to run and scream if a stranger spoke to you. They taught you to be fearful. My husband played a game with my daughter when she was around four years old. He called it the Stranger Danger game. He would be the stranger approaching her in his car. Her role was to respond accordingly. He changed up his temptations, offering her candy, inviting her to pet a puppy, asking her for directions, or saying something to engage her in conversation. She played her part well and ran away from him every time. He made the lesson a game.

However we were taught about stranger danger—to not talk to them, to run away, etc.—it taught us fear.

Then came kindergarten. Your parents took you to the school to prepare you for the day. You walked through the building, you visited your classroom, and maybe you even sat at your desk. And on the first day of school, you stepped onto a bus driven by a stranger. At school you were greeted by another stranger helping you find your classroom. Your teacher was sort of a stranger, as you had met her only once. Throughout the day, you were shuffled from room to room and introduced to more and more strangers. You were surrounded by strangers. You were afraid.

The first day of school scares us to death. The whole experience goes against everything we were taught about safety and strangers. Yet we move forward. We get on that bus. We go to school. We move from classroom to classroom. We hop on the bus again and head home. We find courage. We are brave. We do it, and we do it scared!

Fear evokes a physiological reaction in our body and releases hormones that prepare us to run away from the fear or stay and fight. It's the classic fight-or-flight response. Children on the first day of school have nowhere to run, so they stay.

Our body's physiological reaction to stress, such as an uncomfortable situation, an argument, or being stuck in terrible traffic, is the same as the experience of fear. Hormones are released that prepare us to fight or flee. The end result is that our body does not know the difference between a dangerous situation and one that is simply stressful or uncomfortable. As we grow and mature, either we learn how to process and handle the fearful situation, or we perceive the fear of the stressful situation as dangerous. We learn to fight, or we learn to flee.

I was taught to flee. I was taught to keep my mouth shut, to not the stir the pot, to keep my head down, to do good work, to color within in the lines, and to help those in need. Everything else made me fearful. Something simple, like raising my hand in class, was too much attention for me. It felt scary, so I avoided it.

What causes you fear? What things do you avoid for the sake of staying comfortable? Do you miss opportunities because you are afraid? Does fear make you say no to opportunities to speak or to step up to a new job?

Fear is powerful. Fear can stop us in our tracks. Yet we can learn to face it and move forward. We faced it when we started kindergarten. We can do it again.

JACKIE'S STORY

Let me tell you a story that is the whole reason for this chapter. My daughter, Jackie, was ten years old when I was hospitalized with blood clots covering both lungs. All she knew was her mom was very sick and would be in the hospital for a while. She was afraid. My recovery was long, and I tried to help her feel safe. But, truly, how could I? I could not eliminate her fear. She felt the fear and still moved forward. She didn't let it stop her. She saddled up and finished her school year with a 4.0 grade point average. She thrived academically and athletically. She faced her fears and would not be stopped. One class requirement was to write a paper. She wrote about bravery. Take a read.

BRAVERY

by Jackie Reilly (4ᵗʰ grade)

I was brave. I had to feel good so my mom wouldn't die. I was scared. We talked together and I enjoyed it. I have overheard her talking about how she could have died, how lucky she was to survive blood clots on her lungs. I was brave and scared, but I had to believe she would be okay, and she was. I am crying just writing about it. I feel angry, sad, and lonely. My mom has been through too much. I hate it, but my mom keeps saying, "God still has plans for me." I love her. She is my only mom, and my dad can never replace her. I wish this never happened. She is the best mom in the world. She is getting better, much better. I absolutely hate it. She is my mom. I mean who wouldn't be scared? You have to be brave. Brave enough to write, tell, and think she will be okay, alive and well. She rules.

I invite you to make a shift in the way you face fear. Fear is not something to avoid. In fact, I think it's the exact opposite. Fear is something to recognize and embrace. Pay attention to fear. We feel fear in our gut, otherwise known as the body's second brain, and it's worthy of our attention. Use this information to your advantage.

WHEN YOU FEEL FEAR, EXPLORE THE WHY.

When you feel the fight-or-flight response, what is going on? Is there real danger? Is your safety at stake? Do you need to run? If so, do what you need to do to take care of yourself. But remember, our body doesn't know the difference between dangerous and stressful. So, first recognize why you are feeling what you feel.

When we recognize our fear is from stress or discomfort, then we can get to work. We can use the information to shift how we respond. Just like going to kindergarten, we can feel the fear and do it anyway. When we recognize fear in any situation, we can appreciate the healthy function of our brain to offer the fight-or-flight response—and let it go. Feel the fear and do it anyway.

When I was learning how to swim for my first triathlon, I was scared to death of the water. It's not like I'd ever had a bad experience in the water, but still I feared it. I hated the feeling of my face under the water and not breathing. I had struggled with asthma, bad allergies, and breathing all my life. As a mouth breather, I even struggled with eating and drinking. I cannot tell you how many times I have choked because I was so caught up in a conversation over dinner and inhaled a piece of food. Not pretty. Naturally, when I started swimming, I had panic attacks in the water. I had to keep reminding myself the pool was only four feet deep and I could stand up anytime. This rationale did not change my fear, but I learned to feel the fear and do it anyway. Each time I got in the pool, my heart raced and my hands shook. I didn't let it stop me. I recognized the fear, said *thank you, not now,* and swam anyway.

How do you gain courage? How do you be brave? You might not like my answer, but here it is in the immortal words of Nike: *Just do it.* Take a breath, feel the fear, and plunge in. There is no magic to being brave. You are a kindergarten graduate, so you are already an expert. You can do it again.

TIPS ON BEING BRAVE

What will help you be brave? For me, listening to music works wonders. Science shows that our bodies react to music. The right kind of music induces a positive emotional shift, which then causes a physical shift. When I listen to my favorite songs, I cannot help but move and sing (sometimes to the embarrassment of others watching). It shifts my mood, and it increases my energy, my confidence, and my happiness.

Create a collection your favorite songs. Gather music that makes you feel happy, energized, and uplifted. Keep your music accessible at all times. Whenever you need a little motivation or want to puff up your courage, play your songs. Shift your mood. Shift your body.

I love the movie *Zoolander*. It came out in 2001 with Ben Stiller and Owen Wilson. It's a spoof on the fashion industry, and the star characters are models. When each character enters a scene, his individual theme music plays in the background. Fashion models that they are, they rock the oh-so-confident runway walk. What's your version of this? Be a Zoolander. Decide your theme song, and when you enter a room or enter a big scene, let it play in your head. This will not only help you feel brave but also will keep you in a positive mindset. Stand tall, be brave, and move with the confidence of a supermodel.

Learning how to face my fear and be brave helped me grow as a person, a mom, a wife, and a business owner. I am brave enough to take on leadership roles in major organizations, to speak from the stage, and to write a book.

Ten years ago, I didn't know how to be brave. Today I do. I still feel the fear. I still have to work on being brave, but now I know how. I listen to my music, I feel the fear, I say *thank you not now* as a response, and I do it anyway. I am shifting into happiness, shifting into bravery, shifting into the next opportunity.

It's OK (even natural) to be scared when you try something new. It's OK to be scared when you speak to a room full of strangers. It's OK to be scared when you face your doctor. The trick is to not let that fear stop you. Feel the fear, be brave, and just do it.

ACTION STEPS
to Be Brave

- Create a collection of songs that motivate you. Play them often.

- Feel the fear.

- Acknowledge the fear and say *thank you, not now.*

- Do it anyway.

Chapter 13

FILL YOUR BUCKET

YOU CANNOT POUR FROM
AN EMPTY CUP

What does that mean? Are you someone who loves to support, care for, and nurture others? That requires pouring from your cup all the time. If all you do is give, you empty your cup. Are you open to receiving and replenishing your cup in order to have more to give?

I lead my daughter in a scouting program when she first started school. I loved being around kids and offering lessons to help shape their little minds. One of my tools was a book called *Have You Filled a Bucket Today? A Guide to Daily Happiness for Kids* by Carol McCloud. The basic premise is that we each walk around with a bucket to carry our good thoughts and feelings about ourselves. When our bucket is full, we are happy. When our bucket is empty, we are sad. It's a brilliant lesson that was easy to share with kids.

The message is simple and powerful and as applicable for adults as for kids. It is good to pour happiness from our bucket onto others. It's also good to allow our bucket to be filled. That can be challenging for introverts. If you suffer from low self-esteem, yet you are a nurturer and a giver, it can be challenging for you too. Bucket filling usually goes in one direction. Like the book says, if you are unhappy or lonely, then you need to refill your bucket. I invite you to take bucket filling a step further. Listen to your True Inner Voice and ask what will refill your bucket. What brings you joy?

One technique to fill my introvert cup took some adjusting for me to not feel guilty about it. It takes a lot of energy for me to be the happy introvert when I spend so much time networking, speaking, helping my community, and even socializing with friends. After expending my energy by being around others, I need to recover. Recovery for me is quiet time. A timeout. My timeout is a day with no technology, no phone, no computer, and no communication. I do not talk to people. I relax to watch a string of silly comedies and eat my favorite comfort foods.

On my timeout day, I may or may not shower. I may or may not get out of my pj's. I may or may not brush my teeth. I send my child and my husband away and claim the house for myself. I may not say a word all day. It's wonderful.

Since embracing my skills of public speaking and leadership, I spend more time speaking and leading. That empties my bucket and calls for a refill.

YOUR JOY LIST

What brings you joy? If you don't have a joy list, make one. Everyone needs a joy list! Write down what brings you joy, what activities make you joyful, what makes you giggle, what makes your heart fly, what gets you excited. This is not a bucket list. These are not daydreams of things you will do *someday*. These are things you can run off and do today. Things like going for a run, getting your nails done, having a massage, playing golf. Think road trip. Think hike. Think simple. Think doable. Think today.

Now you have a list of bucket fillers. Post the list in your office or near your phone or on the refrigerator—someplace you will see it daily. On a day when your bucket feels empty, fill it by choosing one of your options for joy. Take it from someone who learned this the hard way: Fill your bucket. Fill your cup.

One of the items on my joy list is riding my horse, BeauJo. If you have never spent time with a horse, come and visit BeauJo. Spending time with a horse feels powerfully majestic and peaceful. When a horse looks into your eyes, he sees your soul. It's amazing to know that this strong, powerful animal simply wants to love me. And when he gets scared, he jumps behind me for protection. Watch your toes!

I didn't grow up with horses. The first time I rode one was on summer vacation. One of the other riders asked how long I had been riding. My answer was ten minutes. He said I was a natural. That was the first time anyone ever said something like that to me. It felt good!

Horses are amazing—large, strong, and fearful of everything. In their company, we need to be completely focused on the task at hand. Whether we are grooming them, leading them down a path, or riding on their back, we need to be completely focused. The to-do lists, the Itty-Bitty Shitty Committee, and the rest of the world need to be put on hold during horse time. I love my horse time.

Make a plan for filling your bucket every day. A full bucket makes you happy. Filling our bucket is one of the easiest things you can do to feel happier, yet so many people don't think to do it. Make a plan to do something daily from your joy list. Start every day with an activity that fills your cup, warms your heart, and makes you the happiest version of you. And if you feel the urge, schedule a timeout once or twice a month.

ACTION STEPS
to Fill Your Bucket

- Create a joy list.

- Do the activities on your joy list.

- Fill your bucket.

Chapter 14

CONCLUSION

Being my own advocate and teaching others to do the same are now my authentic life path. They're also a journey in wellness that requires constant work and attention. Having hitting rock bottom, I have since met so many people who have experienced their own rock bottom. Rock bottom is what flips the switch for people to become their own advocate. I hope my story helps you avoid similar disasters and the lessons from my mistakes help you shift into your total wellness.

MY FINAL EXAM

By now you might be weary of hearing my tales of

emergency rooms and hospitalizations. I get it. But one last story demonstrates my emergence from fear into self-worth.

I put all of my prior lessons to the test in 2016 when I was home alone struggling to breathe and suffering from shooting pain in my back rib. This time, without hesitation, I was on the phone with my doctors, I created an action plan, and I called every single neighbor until one was able to drive me to the hospital. No need for details and specifics here. The end result is I have graduated from being stuck in fear to using my voice and being my own advocate. I am wise and well and worthy!

My journey into wellness and being my own advocate wasn't easy—it began and ended in the hospital. Now that you know my secrets, let's work on this together. Let's start every day with gratitude, embrace our True Inner Voice, speak positively, and work productively with our Committee. Let's use our voice, face our fears, and walk away with gratitude. Let us build our confidence and move toward the life vision that speaks our truth from our core values. Let us pay attention to our progress, celebrate success, be brave, fill others' cups, and remember to take a timeout to fill our own cups.

You are your own best advocate. It's your choice. As

you incorporate the principles in this book, whether you are an introvert and a nurturer like me, an extrovert, or an average Joe, you can make simple shifts to support your advocacy. You are a gift. Today is a gift. Unleash your inner voice and live your best life!

ACTION STEPS
to Unleash Your Inner Voice

- Own the lessons you learn in life and become your best advocate.

- Listen to your True Inner Voice.

- Speak kindly to yourself.

- Speak your truth with your voice.

- Recognize the fear of rejection and remember: It's a choice.

- Be grateful.

- Be confident.

- Live your life vision.

- Celebrate the progress.

- Be brave.

- Fill your bucket.

ACKNOWLEDGMENTS

IN WRITING THIS BOOK, I have learned to be even more grateful for my life, my family, and my voice. A very special thanks to my husband, Tim, who had to live with the good, the bad, and the ugly versions of me. He suggests every future husband run a medical background check on their future spouse. You may or may not want to take his advice.

I would like to thank my entire family for teaching me lessons upon lessons in strength. Thank you to my mother for teaching me to live life with grace. I know you are smiling down from heaven. Thank you to my father for teaching me to laugh often and how to be humble. A special thank you to my sister, Ann Marie, for helping me overcome fear and find the courage to use my voice, my real voice. I know you ALL now wish I would use it less. Keep dreaming.

My shift into owning my greatness is due to working with people smarter than I am. Over the years, I have worked with some amazing coaches and mentors and wish to send a special thank you to Misty, Trey, Tiffany, Kimberly, and Maru. You saw something in me long before I did. Thank you for helping me step there.

Lastly, thank you to Imagine a Moment Photography for capturing my perfect photo.

ABOUT THE AUTHOR

CATHY REILLY is the CEO and Personal Wellness Specialist at Sharing the Shine. She is a keynote speaker, facilitator, and advocacy specialist. After two decades of advocating for others in the litigation arena, Cathy realized most people, including herself, lack the ability to self-advocate. Cathy used her research and fact-finding skills to learn, develop, and master tools to shift her advocacy. Cathy now mentors others on self-advocacy focusing on three critical areas: mind, body, and environment.

Cathy serves on the board for Colorado Business Women and Healthy Denver, Inc. She also serves in a leadership capacity for American Heritage Girls, Troop CO1901 and eWomen Network Denver.

In her spare time Cathy can be found paddle boarding, running outside with her puppy, or romping through the hills of Colorado on her horse, BeauJo.

She currently lives in Denver with her husband, daughter, and beloved animals.

To hire Cathy for facilitated workshops, presentations, or events, you can contact her through:

www.SharingtheShine.com
Facebook: www.facebook.com/sharetheshine
LinkedIn: www.linkedin.com/in/cathyreilly